Praise for Adventure without End

"Richard Bangs is the consummate adventure traveler. He doesn't just see a destination; he finds new ways to discover it. He doesn't just superficially observe a place, he experiences it with a philosophy that has no tolerance for the word 'later.' Is there any better way to go? I think not."

—Peter Greenberg, Travel Editor, NBC Today Show

"Richard Bangs takes trips most of us only dream about. But thankfully his reportage takes us there, and while I'd rather be the guy dining in the Burgundy village of Chambolle-Musigny or admiring the Milky Way on the Inca Trail, I can think of no better proxy than Bangs. His word pictures unveil possibilities that dare us to travel."

—Rudy Maxa, Publisher, Rudy Maxa's Traveler
Host, public television's "Smart Travels" series
Original host, public radio's "Savvy Traveler"
Columnist, MSNBC.com and Expedia.com

"So, there you are minding your business on some Tanzanian backwater when a hippo rises from the depths and lunges at your canoe. What to do? If you're Richard Bangs, quick as a wink, you jam your paddle so far down the beast's throat it's forced into peaceful retreat. As a pioneering member of that growing tribe of adventure travelers, one way or another, he has managed to find his way to virtually all of the wild places on Earth. The experience has been fun but sobering and it's no surprise that he has an urge to talk about it, which he does here with grace, wit, and not an ounce of guile."

—Tom Wallace, Editor-in-Chief, *Condé Nast Traveler*

"Richard Bangs has given us nights filled with shooting stars and days filled with shooting rapids. From Canada's Northwest Territories to Tanzania's hippo-invested waters, from biking Burgundy to hiking Peru's Inca Trail, these captivating adventure chronicles gave me a wicked case of wanderlust. This book is part thrill seeking, part philosophy, and a darn good read."

—Keith Bellows, Editor in Chief, *National Geographic Traveler*

"From jousting with hippos to dancing with crocodiles, Richard Bangs has a way of telling his tales of adventure that prods the dormant explorer in all of us to action."

—Richard Barton, President and CEO, Expedia.com

RICHARD BANGS

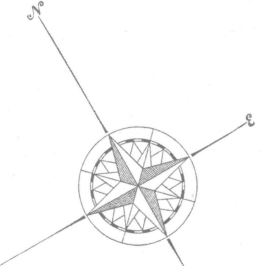

Adventure without End

FOREWORD BY ED VIESTURS

THE MOUNTAINEERS BOOKS

Published by
The Mountaineers Books
1001 SW Klickitat Way, Suite 201
Seattle, WA 98134

First edition, 2001

Published simultaneously in Great Britain by Cordee, 3a DeMontfort Street, Leicester, England, LE1 7HD

Manufactured in the United States of America

Acquiring Editor: Cassandra Conyers
Project Editor: Kathleen Cubley
Editor: Christine Clifton-Thornton
Cover and Book Design: Ani Rucki
Layout: Ani Rucki
Cartographer: Moore Creative Designs
All photographs by Pamela Roberson except page 29 by Jim Laurel, page 37 by Scott Moore, page 49 courtesy Outward Bound International, and page 83 by Russ Sach.

Cover photographs: *Patagonia, Chile* and *Richard Bangs* © Pamela Roberson

Library of Congress Cataloging-in-Publication Data

Bangs, Richard, 1950–
    Richard Bangs, adventure without end / Richard Bangs.— 1st ed.
        p. cm.
    ISBN 0-89886-860-2 (pbk.)
        1. Bangs, Richard, 1950—Journeys. 2. Travel—Anecdotes. I. Title:
    Adventure without end. II. Title.
    G465.B368 2002
    910.4—dc21   2001007165

CONTENTS

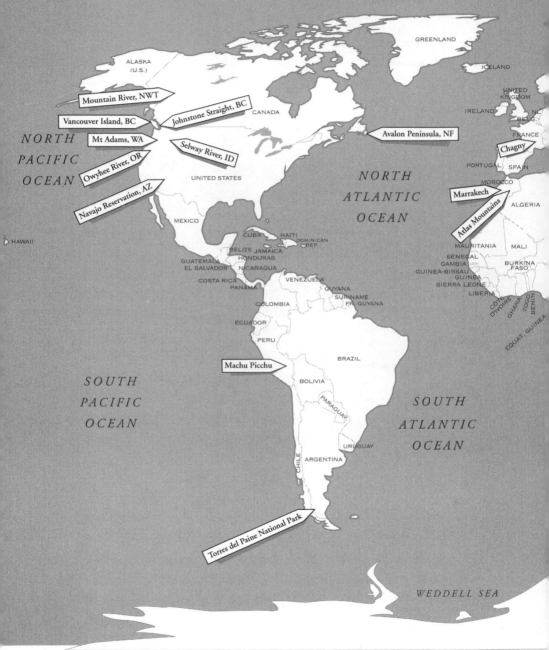

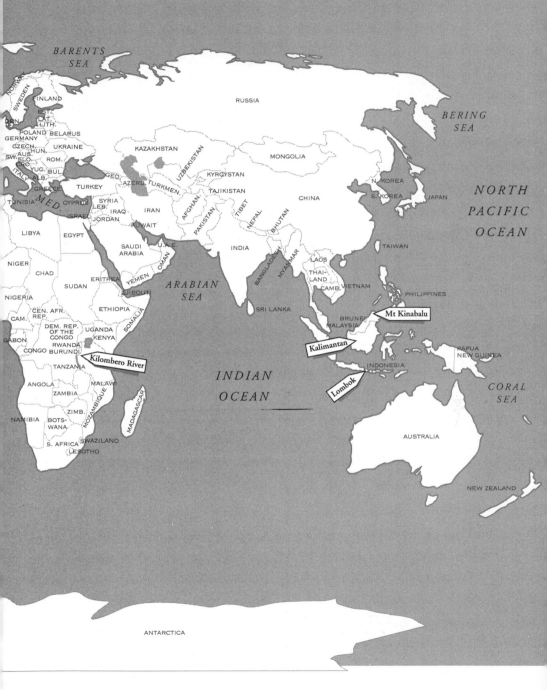

FOREWORD

My first meeting with Richard Bangs occurred in 1996 on the Microsoft campus. It was an introduction concocted by David Roberts, who was writing a profile on me as well as planning to be a correspondent for Richard's online adventure magazine *Mungo Park*. They were about to embark on the first descent of Ethiopia's Tekeze River and David thought that Richard and I should meet.

I had read about and heard of the legendary Richard Bangs— runner of wild, untouched rivers, explorer of distant, tangled jungles, ascentionist of exotic peaks, and founder of the rafting company Sobek. In my mind he was the ultimate adventure guru. An adventurer before adventuring was cool. Adventuring for the sake of slaking a thirst to see what was over the next ridge, beyond the next rapid, or beyond the horizon. Adventuring to have fun and to enjoy the camaraderie of fellow seekers and searchers.

His legacy was that of a global Tom Sawyer: world travel, amazing personal discoveries, extraordinary successes, close calls, and derring-dos. A global map with push pins depicting where he had been would look more like a carpet of quills than a flat surface with an occasional widely-spaced barb.

Upon meeting him I was somewhat humbled by his presence. A soft-spoken bear of a man, his restless energy seemed to surround him like an aura. Wearing his trademark ExOfficio shirt, he seemed always at the ready to grab his toothbrush and plane ticket and walk out the door for points unknown. He was quick to wit and seemed to use an economy of words. He was the definition of the phrase "still waters run deep."

Richard has met more heads of state than most of our presidents—he's a veritable diplomat of adventure. He knew the worth of friendship. People that could open doors to restricted areas, provide guarded escort, assist with permits that could be delayed by the snail's pace of foreign bureaucracy, and provide a cold beer in time of need.

Richard is a conglomerate of Indiana Jones and Walter Mitty. He is the everyman explorer. He has a gift for diving headlong into an untouched corner of the world with only the basic ingredients for adventure—meticulous preparation, unpredictable outcome, a group of friends, a slight naivety, boundless energy, and a gung-ho attitude.

His gear is used, abused, patched, and borrowed. He's been bitten by insects yet to be cataloged by entomologists. He's been bounced by bumpy roads, slogged through quagmires of mud, and felt the inevitable frustrations of travel within foreign countries where bureaucratic disarray is the norm and economy of procedure is rare.

Expedia tales contains a collection of Richard's best writing and adventures. These wonderful stories are penned not only by a visionary and talented adventurer, but also by a gifted and humorous wordsmith. His writings will take you to exotic lands and past the snapping jaws of crocodiles. Escapades, first descents, humorous anecdotes, and joyous discoveries of body and soul—Expedia tales are often lighthearted and comical, but also insightful and sincere. Reading them becomes addictive—like potato chips—try one, and you'll likely need (and want) to read them all. You'll get to know the man that has traveled the world in search of adventure and fun, and through his tales, you'll journey by his side.

—Ed Viesturs

Ed Viesturs is poised to become the first American climber to reach the summit of all the world's 8,000-meter peaks, having climbed thirteen of the fourteen without supplemental oxygen by spring 2001. Viesturs became America's best known high-altitude climber when he appeared in the IMAX film, *Everest*, based on the eventful 1996 spring season there, and the NOVA film project, *Into the Death Zone*. During both film projects, he climbed Everest on cue. Viesturs' feats of high-altitude climbing include his ascent of both Manaslu and Dhaulagiri on a single expedition in the spring 1999, during which he climbed Dhaulagiri alpine-style in three days. For more information about Ed Viesturs, please visit *www.edviesturs.com*.

INTRODUCTION

Oh, give me again the rover's life—the joy, the thrill, the whirl!
Let me leap into thy saddle once more. Let me hear the clatter
of hailstones on icebergs. Let me snuff thee up, sea breeze! And
whinny in thy spray!

Herman Melville

Adventure travel is the anthem of the rover's life, the celebration of
the harmonious confusion of earth and water in a world beyond
the nails of man. The wilderness has always echoed the rover's song
in a thousand voices with profuse strains of unpremeditated art, a
chorus as mixed as a rain forest, yet clear as a river's source.

For twenty-odd years I ran an adventure company called Sobek
Expeditions, guiding friends and clients into the wilds of the world,
illuminating the rover's life, catching the alpenglow of a splendid
peak, the bright blur of a butterfly's flick, the red eyes of a crocodile, the beaded bubbles winking at the rim of a rapid, the scattered
essences of the seasons and seas. It was work made in the heavens,
and I never thought I would leave.

But in 1995 a bright young man named Rich Barton came
calling. He was starting a travel product at Microsoft, an Internet-
based service that would allow people to research and book any
travel anywhere in the world, including adventures, grand and tall.
He asked if I would come north to Redmond and work with him,
creating an adjacent site that would celebrate adventure and then
allow those inspired to act upon the inspiration and plunge in. It

11

seemed intriguing, but I was glad with my lot, transforming lives in powerful ways through travel and adventure. But Rich is a persuasive soul, and along with some of his associates—Nathan Myhrvold, Greg Slyngstad, Patty Stonesifer, Erik Blachford, and Melinda French Gates—he convinced me to leave Sobek behind and come work with him, helping to change the world of travel yet staying true to my spirit.

So in 1996 I moved to the Great Northwest and launched a product called *Mungo Park*, an online interactive magazine that organized and led expeditions each month around the globe and covered them in real time via the Internet. It was a wonderful project, and for two years imagination was the only limitation.

But the dream didn't last. The project was expensive, and the Internet audience was not yet ready for the type of rich content and interactivity that are hallmarks of an online adventure travel magazine. So *Mungo Park* was parked, and Rich Barton asked me to work with him at the larger initiative, *Expedia.com*. Again, I wondered if I would be drifting away from my own mission of discovery, sharing, and empowering. But Rich assured me otherwise, and I became Editor-at-Large for Expedia. And what a magnificent post it has been.

The public relations folks like to say Expedia is made up of travelers. They are right, and I have been Exhibit A. In the five years I worked with Rich Barton, I circled the globe as many times and designed and partook in a score of adventures. I wrote about these experiences for *Mungo Park,* for *MSNBC.com,* and for Expedia. The collection of stories herein is culled from these writings, and in total they celebrate the profound goodness, the joy and bliss, of travel and adventure. And though Expedia enables all who travel, from those on business to those in search of a romantic getaway, it has always had a big heart for those in search of adventure.

And for good reasons. As Mark Twain said, travel is fatal to prejudice and bigotry, and while all travel is good, adventure travel is on the fine edge of the scale. It celebrates diversity, and the goal is discovery, enlightenment, and all manner of personal challenge—

intellectual, physical, cultural, and even spiritual. This embracing of diversity represents a positive evolution toward a higher consciousness. The first principle of the science of ecology is that uniformity in any system is unstable and unhealthy, while, conversely, diversity is the singular attribute of a healthy, stable system. Seeking out and fostering diversity in the natural world and among human cultures is a most significant characteristic of adventure travel. The best way to instill an appreciation of the wonderful diversity of this planet is to experience it firsthand. Then the appreciation becomes more than just academic; it becomes emotional as well. To someone who has truly gained such an appreciation, it is not necessary (or sufficient) to justify protection of wild spaces or endangered archeological sites in terms of discounted net value of revenue flows from tourism versus those from natural resource exploitation. The nonmaterial benefits of protecting these special spots may be intangible (in a material sense), but they are very real—and they are priceless and irreplaceable.

Adventure travelers are active versus passive, in that the traveler takes an active role in creating the experience. In most cases just getting there requires active participation, such as rafting, hiking, or kayaking. And the active traveler is the traveler most likely to act, to take an issue position having once been exposed to a threatened environment, and to dedicate time, energy, money, and voice to saving what now has personal meaning. Such is the moral imperative behind adventure travel. With firsthand experience comes appreciation, acknowledgement of worth and respect, and a desire and a reason to preserve the Earth's bounty. The Colorado River still flows through the Grand Canyon, the salmon still run up the Rogue, Walden Pond still reflects, the wildlife of Tanzania still roams—all in part because of the softly stepping visitors who liked what they saw and experienced, learned about the issues, and subsequently got involved.

Adventure travelers must know that it is impossible to visit an environment, a culture, without taking some toll on the land. But it is the larger ledger that must be considered. Every inch of the planet has been charted, inspected, and lusted after by commercial or governmental concerns and, most often, if left alone, unvisited, these places fall to the short-term exploitation of industrial and business enterprises. Unfortunately, in many cases, nobody notices until it's too late. But when adventure travelers come around—the active traveler, the rafter, the kayaker, the backpacker—they become an active constituent and a powerful voice for a better way. They leave behind money in a local economy, which improves a way of life, while at the same time celebrating tradition; they fight to keep the wild places so, as they have been personally touched by the alchemy and beauty of pristine places and want to return, even if just in memory.

We all float in this single cell called Earth. By exploring the wealth of our wilds, by venturing forth into the wilderness, we embrace beauty full of healing and strength, inject a pulsing in our spirits and blood, and make the earth and ourselves better for it.

So let the rivers roll to waft us, the sun to light our rise. Use the Earth as a footstool to touch the canopy of the skies. Leap into the saddle, share in the joy, the thrill, and whinny in the spray. Ride, as I did in these pages, through the meadows and streams, the mountains and canyons, appareled in light, and journey the wild places as glorious as the freshness of a dream, into a bold world of travel and adventure without end.

—Richard Bangs

HIPPO HOLIDAYS

HIPPO HOLIDAYS

The Broad-back hippopotamus
Rests on his belly in the mud;
Although he seems so firm to us
He is merely flesh and blood.

T. S. Eliot
"The Hippopotamus," 1920

As is not uncommon on raft trips, we were lolling about in a glassy section, singing a Simon and Garfunkel song, watching the notes disappear into the passing myombo trees. I pulled the oars to the rhythm of the song, lost in a reverie.

Then, a lumbering flash. The raft reared, and my note shot an octave. A hiss spat from the stern as a chamber collapsed like a punctured lung. Suddenly, all was quiet. The heat was pierced by a chill. Overhead a cormorant rode an updraft. Then the attacker emerged —a great gray hulk, water washing from its head like off a whale's back. Tiny, turreted eyes flared as its mouth stretched like a steam shovel with teeth. It lunged, and instinctively I lifted the ten-foot oar and jabbed its blade into the fleshy, saliva-rimmed maw. The animal bit the oar, twisted, then as I pushed the blade as far into its throat as I could, it let out a bellow then sank into the depths, leaving just a swirl on the surface as its signature.

"Kiboko gone," Majiji, a retired crocodile hunter and local guide, announced. *Kiboko,* I learned, is Swahili for hippopotamus.

In the cabinet of wonders, I had reached for the top shelf on a safari of a different sort. I had joined as a raft guide on an expedition that would float the Kilombero and Rufiji Rivers, through the Selous, the largest uninhabited game reserve in the world, spreading across a giant swath of Tanzania. Its 21,000 square miles make it larger than the central African counties of Burundi and Rwanda combined and almost four times as large as Serengeti National Park to the north. But while the Selous contains some of the largest concentrations of big game in Africa (an estimated 100,000 elephant), and is one of the oldest, having been established by Germans in 1905, it is easily the least visited by humans. Its lack of facilities, and the government's ambivalent attitude toward tourism development, has kept it quiet. Huge tracks of the reserve remain untramped by shoed feet, unseen by Western eyes. It is one of the rare plots of earth that has survived unchanged since pre-history, due in large part to its infertile soil and tsetse fly populations—factors that discourage human settlement.

I had spent the year previous behind a desk in a city and found myself hungering for the wild, for a place where wildlife reigned, where the canons were unbound. I was at a still point in the turning world, was a periphrastic study in a worn-out fashion, too still with intolerable wrestlings. I decided I needed a raid into Africa and a journey down the strong brown god of a river that ran through the Selous.

Its namesake is Frederick Courtenay Selous, a British elephant hunter who claimed 1,000 big-game trophies and who guided the likes of Cecil Rhodes and Theodore Roosevelt through the region. He died while leading an attack on the Germans in 1917 near the Rufiji River and was posthumously prized with the Distinguished Service Order and a game reserve in his name, the latter in 1922 after the British conquest of Tanganyika.

The odyssey began at the agricultural settlement of Ifakara, just beyond the western boundary of the reserve and a stop on the Chinese-built Tazara Railway. Along with veteran guide Bart Henderson, I arrived a couple days earlier than most of the group to prep the boats—four hypalon inflatables that needed frames. The choice was whether to build the frames from sturdy, hardwood planks from the nearby Swiss Catholic Mission workshop, or from the more fragile but aesthetic bamboo.

"Let's go native," Bart beseeched. And six hours later we stood over a latticework of bamboo crafted to carry a varied assortment of gear, from fifty-caliber ammunition boxes holding our cameras to reed baskets holding fresh fruit and vegetables.

The rest of the group caught up on schedule, and in a driving rain we loaded and launched the expedition on the Rumemo River, a small tributary that runs through Ifakara. Amidst the shrieks of the villagers we made our first strokes and swirled southward, away from orthodoxy, into the dark way of ignorance.

Almost immediately the Rumemo began to braid through a quagmire of elephant grass, channels dividing into ever-shallower channels. The boats slugged to a stop in stagnant water, and the game scouts leapt into the mucky water and started slashing the grass with *pangas,* wrenching the rafts through the swamp. To me, the reedy water looked like a crocodile refuge, but not wanting to be upstaged by the local talent I vaulted into the water as well and started towing one of the rafts, a la Humphrey Bogart in *The African Queen,* leeches and all.

A few hours later we emerged into the open waters of the Kilombero, and the most impressive feature was the beat of the sun. The landscape was almost featureless, an endless expanse occasionally dotted with a dohm palm. A couple miles downstream a primitive ferry operation, with a thatched roof for shade, drew us in for a respite. As we staggered to the shade, steaming tulip glasses filled with hot tea were thrust into our hands, as seems to be the custom in many parched areas of the world.

Slaked, but not cooled, we pushed off, and as we drifted downstream the river and its surroundings began to assume a more extravagant character. Distant mountains wavered into focus, the riverside vegetation increased, and a few hippos showed their snouts. Camp, our first on the river, was a broad beach pockmarked with hippo footprints and ringed with African sounds—the eerie wail of hyenas, the whoop of lions, and the whine of mosquitoes.

The next several days the flotilla slid deeper into authentic Africa. Evidence of humanity faded and in inverse proportions wildlife presented itself—elephant, crocodiles, fish, eagles, Cape buffalo, zebra, giraffe, waterbuck, wildebeest, and impala, a faithless parade of game. Hippos, however, ruled this world; we passed four hundred on the fourth day. I was on a river gauntlet, maneuvering through a field of mammalian land mines. As we negotiated downriver, the hippos reared up, snorted, and bellowed, stretching mandibles that could swallow a man whole. But, their dangerous miens notwithstanding, there was a poetry to their movements. They sometimes seemed to be dancing, in some choreographed and orchestrated way. Until the one that bit my boat. . . . Afterwards, cute they never seemed again.

That night as we patched the punctured raft, there was talk of close calls in Africa. Bart related how, a month earlier, he was in Ethiopia gathering gear for this expedition when he was invited to join a New Year's Day drive to the Awash Park for a picnic. A hangover, however, kept him from the date on the morning of departure, and as he rolled about in his bed, the Land Rover was attacked and two of the picnickers were shot dead.

Morning brought a blither mood, and downstream we passed into a lush vegetation belt. Green and motion somehow makes the soul lighter. Zebra scattered and reedbuck bounced along the banks. At lunch, Majiji lustily reeled in a six-foot Vundu catfish, a delight, since he and the other game scouts loathed our freeze-dried food.

Hippo density increased with each mile. Mike Ghilglieri, a zoologist with a specialty in African fauna, had been keeping tabs, and by late afternoon announced we had passed two thousand. Moments later, another surfaced inches behind a boat piloted by seasoned river guide Jim Slade—and it ferociously shook its head and harrumphed.

"Paddle hard. *Paddle very hard!*" Slade screamed to his crew, and the raft rocketed away. With the danger past, we gathered at the bank for a breather and found the back of Slade's shirt coated with hippo mucus. Enough excitement for one day, so it seemed. We made camp.

Sunday was malaria pill day. Once a week we all gathered for the ritual downing of a 200-milligram malaria prophylaxis tablet that kept the sporozoan parasites from the bites of anopheline mosquitoes inactive. It was also the day of portages.

The first was around the upper Shiguri Falls, a mile-long stretch of river broken by a score of cataracts created by ancient lava flows. We rolled up our gear into manageable pieces and began the trek through the savannah, along hippo trails thick with acacias, hedgehogs, cheval-de-frise, and other vegetable matter that resembled barbwire. Down this thorny route we rattled, balancing buckets, duffels, and boating paraphernalia on our heads, African porter style. The rafts were carried inflated, three bearers on each side, an awkward task that had me stumbling along hunched and half-blind from the streaks of sweat across my glasses.

After the third boat was wrestled through the portage, Jim Slade made a suggestion: "Let's see if we can run this last boat through at least to the lip of the main falls of this section." Bart would have nothing to do with it; he'd witnessed far too many boating accidents in his years as a river guide. But seven of us, senses dulled from the exhaustion of the carries, agreed to make the run.

It took an hour to scout the run, more time than the foot portage. But with the route firmly etched in mind, six paddlers launched into the froth of upper Shiguri Falls. Convincing myself that discretion was the greater part of survival, I volunteered to stand at the lip of the main falls, some 200 yards downstream from the casting-off point, with a coiled rescue line in case they missed their mark. Tense as a pulled bow, I stood ready to sling the rope to my friends when they appeared. I couldn't see their approach, as the jungle stretched deep into the mainstream; I couldn't hear them for the roar of the falls. So I waited. Three minutes—the rope felt like sponge from my sweat; five minutes—my eyes began to sting from the salt pouring down my brow; six minutes—the raft caromed into sight around a midstream island, pointed directly at me. I wound up and flung the rope, but before it uncoiled to its length, the boat rammed into the shore at my feet, and six triumphant souls stepped out.

Midafternoon we were rerigged and bumping downstream toward the second piece of Shiguri Falls—the ticklish part. The current was fast here, and spirits soared as we sailed through a rain forest, lush and alive. As the least in shape of the guides I was pulling up the rear when, from the left bank a particularly large hippo, disturbed by the preceding boats, splashed into the river and instinctively galloped for deep water. Alas, his path to sanctuary intersected with mine toward the main current channel. As hard as I could I pushed on the oars, trying to speed the raft in the rapids; the hippo, panicked, was running faster. My boat skimmed; the hippo splashed. At the head of the channel I was in front, barely, and glanced over my shoulder to see the hippo just three feet from the stern, his giant jaws clacking like some industrial shovel. Only the thin rubber of the raft and our flimsy bamboo frame separated us from the beast bearing down on us. With a last adrenaline surge I pumped the oars, but the raft hung on a rock.

"Brace," I yelled to the crew—and the world shattered with a thunderous crack. The hippo got the boat, I thought. But I swung around and saw Majiji in the stern, lowering his 30.06 rifle. In a boil of crimson and russet water, the hippo, with a hole between its stunned eyes, rolled and sank.

Sighs, short and frequent, were exhaled. We were in shock. Up to this point, the close encounters with hippos had been almost theme-park-like adventures; they popped in and out of our lives and sent our blood racing. Now, though, a line had been crossed, a life lost. The hippo, a gentle giant in most scenarios, a vegetarian who keeps to himself, was only trying to escape perceived danger into the protection of deep water—and we had stilled him, for the sake of our little escapade. Africa has many cunning passages and contrived corners, and survival of the fittest is more evident here than almost anywhere else. But, guided by vanities, I thought we were above the base rules of this continent. Now I saw that, between the idea and the reality, between the motion and the act, the shadow fell. We were as much a part of Africa as its beasts.

The episode weighed on us as we pulled in to begin the next portage, a four-mile hump around the main of Shiguri Falls. It took over three hours to carry a load one way, and we needed ten loads to move the complement. On the first march, as we wended down a hippo trail, Majiji stopped us midstride and put his finger to his mouth. Through a mesh of kigelia trees we saw a colossal elephant with tusks like warped poles digging at the umber earth. Two lesser pachyderms mimicked the motions right behind. Though just a few trunk-lengths away, they didn't sense our presence until Majiji pulled out an elephant whistle and wailed away. With the nettling noise they flapped their droopy ears, rotated on their hind legs, and trundled away up the steep hillside.

Where the Luwegu River joins the Kilombero to create the Rufiji, we dropped the last of our portage loads after three hard days of carrying. And it was with relief that we pushed the rafts back into the brown waters.

The temperament of the river changed dramatically here; it was now narrow and swift, lined with ficus trees and Colobus monkeys. Pied kingfishers flitted about the boats. A herd of Cape buffalo wallowed in an eddy around one bend, and waterbuck posed regally on a beach around another; two lions lolled in the grass around still another. And the crocodiles were now out in leagues; we counted twenty-seven in the first hour. One surfaced two feet from Jim Slade and he clubbed it over the head with his paddle.

For two days we gyred down the Rufiji to the confluence with the Great Ruaha, which assumed the legend thereafter. A polished and fluted limestone canyon marked the beginning of Steigler's Gorge (named after a German big-game hunter stomped to death by an elephant), a twenty-mile section torn by rapids of questionable navigability. We knew from our pre-expedition meetings with the American Embassy in Dar es Salaam that a small safari camp was just a few miles inland above the gorge, and that it harbored a

Cessna, so Jim Slade and I volunteered to hike to the camp to see if we might arrange an aerial reconnaissance of the rapids before we pitched our boats into the gorge.

Jim and I reeled into the Steigler's Gorge camp just in time for a dinner of barbecued impala and cold beer with Andrew, the Canadian director of the facility and a Waldo Pepperish pilot. He regaled us deep into the night, licked by campfire light, telling tales of life in the Selous bush—the spitting cobra found in a client's toilet bowl (wearing sunglasses to protect his eyes, Andrew whacked away half-blind in the half-light, skiving more toilet seat than snake); the hippo that attacked his fiberglass Boston Whaler full of blue-haired tourists and took out a steak-size chunk of his Johnson outboard; and the time he went skinny dipping at the entrance to Steigler's Gorge on a family picnic and slipped and was swept into the rapids. His parents had given him up for drowned when, two hours later, he appeared shinnying nude along the cliffs back to the picnic site.

A night of battling fleas in one of the camp cots made an early rise easy. By dawn we were taxiing down the dirt strip, ground hornbills scattering, Andrew steering with his knees as he tried to wipe the windshield with his tee shirt. Then we were off the ground, winging over Africa. In greater numbers than ever before I saw elephant, antelope, and buffalo—even a couple rhino, the horned tank-like beasts on the edge of extinction. In minutes we were over the gorge, a crooked gash through the skin of the savannah. From the air the rapids looked big but navigable. In a couple hours we were back at the rafts, rigging for heavy white water, double-tying all the gear, checking and rechecking the panoply of knots.

Off we pushed. The sound was barely audible at first, then it rose to a roar as the rafts slid into the gorge. We tugged lifejackets tighter. At the gateway, the river seemed to drop off into space. We could see occasional jets of water dancing like tongues of white flame on the surface.

At the lip we looked down into a mix of standing waves,

yawning holes, whirlpools, and fast eddies. The bow of my boat dropped as though it were the first car of a roller coaster at the apex; a second later it jumped toward the sky. Spreading streamers of spray seemed to hover above me like fireworks, then the shock of water washed over me. The raft shuddered from the impact, recovered, then met the next one, *wham, wham, wham.* All I could see between drenchings was a kaleidoscope of white water, black cliffs, blue sky, and flying spray. Ten minutes later we were through, bobbing in the tail waves.

For a moment I gazed down a river corridor that widened and narrowed and opened back again to reveal terraced rock temples against the sky, sculpted by wind and water over millions of years. On one wall were classical columns and cornices, and a series of horizontal slabs straight from a Frank Lloyd Wright prairie house; on another wall, exposed schists resembled Henry Moore sculptures, polished like black marble by the silty waters.

Below the gorge the Great Ruaha slackened and meandered into a forest of dead palm trees, victims of a sudden channel change in the river during a flood a couple years back. We eased through a graveyard of topless, bleached trees, counting the last few hippos and pulling the last strokes on the oars as we emerged into Lake Tagalala, our take-out. A Land Rover packed with fresh fruit and tepid beer welcomed us and drove us to a nearby hot springs for a soak. As I draped over a piece of travertine, chest-high in the mineral water, Michael Ghilglieri made a summary: "Three-thousand, five-hundred eighty-six—our final hippo count. That translates to approximately a million pounds of meat—less than New York City eats in one day."

An interesting factoid. But it was more information than I wanted to know, and I slid my entire body under the warm water and washed away the heaps of broken images of hippos, letting the liquid shiftings bathe away the stains of the river, allowing me back to a world less wild.

DOWN THE
CRAZY RIVER

BLACKFEATHER RIVER, NORTHWEST TERRITORIES, CANADA
*Our small party of paddlers negotiates the chilly waters of this
remote river in the Canadian far north, accessible only a few
short weeks in summer.*

DOWN THE CRAZY RIVER

He who paddles two canoes, sinks.

Anonymous African (Bemba) proverb

The primary response is one of exhilaration, the splendid frisson that comes with gliding by the edge.

We were on a river so remote it doesn't appear on most maps, the Blackfeather, a tributary of the Mountain River, deep in the Mackenzie Mountains of Canada's Northwest Territories, about one hundred miles south of the Arctic Circle. These are wilderness waterways in the truest sense. The courses have no impoundments, no diversion projects, no bridges, no roads, no homes, no people, no pollution. The Mountain Dene people once hunted and trapped here, but they long ago moved to villages on the Mackenzie, and now the only remnant is a void. These rivers flow, as they have since time immemorial, in balance with themselves. The Blackfeather and Mountain, and every rill that feeds them, are in unmodified natural states. If they belong to anyone, they belong to the wildlife, superbly adapted to this inimical region: moose, wolf, wolverine, Dall sheep, mountain caribou, beaver, and grizzly bear. My canoe mate was my friend Erik, the marketing director for Expedia.com, the Web-based travel service. The other in our party was our part-time male model guide Bart, who was making his first descent. Our plan was to catch up with four others—two brothers, Peter and Paul; Erik's dad, John; and our master guide, Tim, at twenty-two a veteran of many northern river trips, who had launched the day before us.

To get to our river we first flew commercially to the oil pipe-line community of Norman Wells on the Mackenzie River. From there we boarded a Swiss-made Pilatus PC-6 Porter, a STOL (short take-off and landing) floatplane, often called the "Jeep of the air." The high-winged, angular black-and-yellow Porter took us farther north and east into an intermontane basin in the Mackenzie Range, over a spot of water that looked like a human eye brooding. It seemed to mirror the soul of the landscape. We splashed down on Willow-handle Lake, at about 4,000 feet. The air is usually the first sign that you are someplace different, but here, as we stepped off the pontoons, it was the light—soft, diffuse, and intense all at once. The air, too, made its point. It was autumn cold, and I looked to the south for a piece of last warmth before the sun made its last horse-shoe pass around the margins of the sky.

Because of schedule conflicts, the rest of the party had launched the previous day. Erik and I climbed into one canoe, Bart in the other, and together we took off sliding across the glasslike lake, all silent except for the periodic calls of loons echoing across the canyon, and the swish of water as it broke across the hull. At the far end we hoisted the canoes and kits on our heads and backs and began a kilometer portage along a faint track littered with fresh grizzly tracks. We made camp at a creek called Push-Me-Pull-You. As we turned our canoe over to become our makeshift dinner table, I saw the bottom scored with a matrix of scratches and dents, the scars from a season in tough waters.

The next day we loaded the boats and proceeded to push and pull them down a water passage not much bigger than a garden-hose rivulet. It was back-breaking work in stinging-cold water, which lasted all morning. Eventually the trickle conflued with the Blackfeather, and there was at last the thrill of a live vessel beneath us riding high over brawling water—until the boat began to crankle as though drunk, and our misadventures began.

The river is fast at this point, and the paddles swallow yards with each stroke. We stretch to pull into an eddy, but can't make it. Even though we have spray covers over the seventeen-foot red canoe, and just bailed the boat dry less than ten minutes ago, water is splashing about my knees and the canoe is reeling like a sailboat in a squall. "We've got a leak in the boat," Erik yells from behind. But no time to ponder that information . . . just ahead the river roils, and we need a quick decision. To the right is a waterfall; down the center is a washboard running with white ribs of foam; to the left is a narrow channel between an anvil-shaped rock and the shore.

"To the left," I scream back to Erik while turning the bow. We line up, and slew a good line to make the chute. Zen and the art of canoeing: I can feel my arms connected to the water and my mind to Erik's strokes behind me, and instinctively know what to do. The entry seems perfect, gliding toward the chute as though on a track, slipping down the drop as though by design. Then, a hidden hand seems to reach down, grab the boat, and push us back toward the Paleozoic rock.

I drop my paddle, brace against the gunnels, and *BANG*—we crash head-on into the stone. It stops us cold, and the canoe shudders, then wobbles back into the mainstream, miraculously upright, skidding on a crackling surge of spume. I can see two new holes in the bow. Water is swishing around my belly. We try to keep the canoe straight as we head into the tall waves, but it's like steering an overflowing bathtub. Instead of riding over the crests, we plow through them. When we spot our guide, Bart, downstream, we wag our paddles like semaphores, but he is too busy negotiating his own boat through the quicksilver to notice our distress. We're on our own.

Somehow we make it to a shallow eddy by the cobblestone bank and jump out into the icy water in our sandals. The air is dank as an oyster. Clouds fill the sky and seal us off, enforcing a sense of claustrophobia.

We'd hoped to catch up to the other group, but in our current condition, the prospects don't look good. A short way up the loamy shore is a blanket of snow, and beyond, cliffs that soar half a mile high. We have no patching material, no detailed maps, food for only a few days, and the sun is beginning to fade behind the brooding peaks. The outfitter had supplied us with lifejackets that are little more than sports bras, a size too small, good to ninety pounds, which we are not. And Tim had the duct tape, which can patch almost any hole in a canoe. Ours is the last scheduled trip of the short season, so there's no chance of someone paddling to our rescue. And we can't camp here, as we had been warned by an earlier group that there had been a caribou kill by a grizzly nearby; if we pitched in the vicinity we might become bear pops.

As we bend to bail the canoe, Erik and I exchange a stern look. There is an ancient silence, as unbroken as the flow of the river, and I feel a bead of fear in my gut—but suddenly we both snap to a smile. "I can't think of any place in the world I would rather be," I offer to Erik. "Yup . . . we're canoeing!" he practically sings.

There is nothing quite as satisfying as messing about in a canoe, and it gets better as the setting gets wilder and warmer as the flame of risk burns brighter. When the late Bill Mason, Canada's quintessential riverman, said that nothing was quite as perfect as a canoe, he of course meant that perfection is attained not when there is no longer anything to add, such as in a rich man's yacht, but when there is no longer anything to take away, when a craft has been stripped down to its nakedness. With our boat stripped of some of its skin, we were negotiating a vessel beyond perfection.

Now, as we bail the last gallons from the bilge, we assess our predicament. "Maybe we could tap some sap from the spruce trees and use it to patch the boat," Erik wonders aloud. I love the idea, and suggest we camp and make an attempt to fix the canoe, bears be damned. But it would probably take a full day to make such a repair, which would cut the chances of catching up with our group to near impossible. Erik insists we make as much distance as possible during daylight, and then explore the options. A part of me is drawn to the notion of trying to negotiate through this wilderness on foot, on a mission of survival, no itinerary, no planned meals, no accoutrements to weigh down the soul, just a clear, present reason for going forward, for being. But I know Erik holds out hope for our meeting up with his Dad and the others, and it is the right thing to do.

We relaunch, and it starts to rain. I look around. In the way that beach stones are more colorful when wet, the rain brings out the colors of the land, and for a minute I am entranced. The limestones and dolomites are buff and cinnamon, the shales a shiny black, the siltstones green, the sandstone maroon. Above, a golden eagle whooshes like a prehistoric bird. Then I plunge back into the reality pudding. The canoe is full again, rolling like a three-ton log, nearly capsizing at every turn; we stop and bail, paddle for fifteen minutes, and then repeat again and then again. The wind is whipping the rain around like wet string. It's so cold my whole body is shivering, and whenever a shot of water meets my face it punches my breath away. My feet feel like they were used for batting practice. My mind is numbing from the exercise. Then, just as I find myself surveying the cliffs for an exit trek, we turn a corner and the Blackfeather makes its final adjustments, like a settling stomach, and then merges into the murky waters of the Mountain River. There, across the channel, is an orange and white tarp, rigged like a sail, with men milling about beneath—our rendezvous, our deliverance.

My feelings are . . . mixed. . . . It will be exciting to be with fellow adventurers, and to meet Erik's dad; and it will be a comfort to be with an expert guide who knows the river and has all the tools to make the rest of the trip ideal. But for half a day, as Erik and I made our way with our leaky red canoe down a river of liquid lightning, there was a sensation, an alertness, a primal freedom, that comes with reducing existence to its core in the unavailing wilderness, challenging it on its own terms, and being a bit scared. Looking back at the needles of light flashing off the Blackfeather, I knew that we were leaving the fear of the unknown behind. In a 1757 essay, "Of the Sublime and Beautiful," Edmund Burke argued that the sublime began with a proper sense of dread; only terror "is a source of the sublime; that is, it is productive of the strongest emotion which the mind is capable of feeling." And even though each final stroke of the day was dissipating to shining ether the solid angularity of our earlier predicament, I lock it to memory, and let a wave of joy wash over me. As we sailed for the rendezvous, I patted our canoe on its cheek. It had such a lovely place to run, and all downhill.

KRAKAUER'S CURSE

KRAKAUER'S CURSE
The Second Mountain Syndrome

T oo many sailors drive the boat up the mountain.

Anonymous Japanese proverb

It seems in the wake of *Into Thin Air,* Jon Krakauer's wildly success-ful account of the Everest disaster of May 1996, everyone wants to climb Mount Everest. But the phenomenon has spread beyond the world's highest peak to Alaska's Denali, highest in North America; Argentina's Aconcagua, highest in South America; Kilimanjaro, Africa's crown; and even Mount Rainier, highest in the northwestern United States.

Whatever it is about the highest ground that storms about our national consciousness and elevates these rocks to icon status, it is not raining water that lifts all boats. While the light of allure has intensified on these primary peaks, those second in command have remained relatively unnoticed and untrammeled. Among mountain-eering cognoscenti, Pakistan's K2 (8,611 meters) is considered a more challenging peak than Everest (and more beautiful), but the man on the street has never heard of the Karakorum great. And while Sir Edmund Hillary, the "conqueror of Everest," is a name known by millions, it would be rare to find anyone who can cite the men who first crested K2 (Italians Achille Compagnoni and Lino Lacedelli, who summited July 31, 1954).

Most Americans know of Mount McKinley (or its Native American name, Denali), but few can identify Mount Logan (6,052 meters) in the Yukon as the continent's second tallest peak. Many who have considered climbing a mountain have heard of Aconcagua (6,959 meters), highest in the Western Hemisphere, but who has heard of Chile's Ojos del Salado (6,880 meters), the honorable number two? Quick: What's the next highest peak in Africa after Kilimanjaro (5,963 meters)? It's the more formidable Mount Kenya (5,291 meters), never a part of Hemingway's mythology.

In the northwestern United States, the volcano known as Rainier gets all the notice. It rafts above Seattle's bounding clouds and was once the training ground for American Everest climbers. And it has seen record numbers of climbers the last few years, unabated despite a recent death in an avalanche. Even before the current wave of mountain adventurers, inspired by the Everest disaster and its never-ending media coverage, came onto the scene, Rainier was an increasingly popular climb. I did the deed in 1995 and was dismayed at the sheer numbers on the slope. I had to wait in line at certain points and jockey for position at others. I shared the summit moment with a score of strangers and, on the descent, dropped into place with all the others like ants marching down an ice-cream cone. Its remote access notwithstanding, it was not a wilderness experience.

Mountains, like rock stars, can have celebrity. And when some tipping point brings a mountain into popular consciousness, people flock to the icon to bask in the shadow of a star. Usually the highest mountain in a range achieves this lofty state just because it is the lead, and as such draws the most traffic. The second-highest just doesn't get the attention, and often then is the better wilderness experience.

For this reason I set out to explore the Northwest's second-highest mountain, Mount Adams (3,758 meters). I discovered a passage as impressive as its bigger sister and a white wilderness clean, mean, and seldom seen, at least in relation to the region's celebrity mountain, Rainier, to the north.

After a six-hour drive from Seattle, we convened at the Bird Creek Meadows trailhead, about a mile high on the southern skirt of Mount Adams, within the Yakama Indian Reservation. The Indians long worshipped Adams as Pah-to, son of the Great Spirit Klickitat, and in legend linked the peak in a fraternal battle with Wy-east (Mount Hood), over the courtship of Loo-wit (Mount St. Helens). I had put together the trip with a group of friends and, to guide us, had hired Mountain Madness, the company founded by the late Scott Fisher, the über-guide Jon Krakauer reproved in *Into Thin Air* for fatally leading the suboptimally experienced group up Everest. Now the company is under new ownership, Chris and Keith Boskoff, both Himalayan veterans, and Chris is on an ambitious path to become the first woman to climb all fourteen 8,000-meter peaks.

We were a trailmix of experience, from Pasquale Scaturro, who had just summited Everest in May and was on a busman's holiday, to the tyros, a couple of writers who had never been camping. With sixty-pound packs snugly shouldered, we headed up the hill. As instructed by one of our guides, twenty-three-year-old Cecilia Martenson, we stepped lightly through the brooding evergreens and past fields of huckleberries, being careful to stay on the trail. The trees gave way to subalpine mountain meadows, where several marmots, perched trailside, were fattening themselves on flowers. When we stopped to fatten ourselves after a couple hours on the trail, I pulled back the wrapper on a chocolate energy bar only to reveal a squirming knot of milk-colored maggots, and most appetites seized. The exception was Matt Stonesifer, who had just returned from a solo wilderness excursion in the southwest, and had tasted maggots and found them to be "okay." He talked knowingly of their high nutritional value, delighting in our squeamishness.

We made an early camp above Hellroaring Creek at 2,000 meters, a mere fingertip away from the bright volcanic crown, high and lordly as a god. High above us the frosty fingers of Klickitat and Rusk Glaciers gripped the cone of Adams, forming a wonderland of wide snowfields, crevasses, snow bridges, gleaming seracs, bergshrunds, and awesome icefalls. It was fantastic and frightening.

Though this was August, height of the Northwest climbing season, and we were just a few miles from the parking lot, we had passed but a single couple on the hike and were now seemingly utterly alone. I looked around while supping on our campfire-cooked Thai dinner and sipping Starbucks and saw not a sign of anyone nor anything not wild. Krakauer's influence had not found this space. As if to punctuate the thought, I heard the distant mumbling of an avalanche somewhere up the mountain. Its voice sounded hollow, tubular, and for a moment I felt like we were camped in the barrel of a very large gun.

The night was filled with shooting stars, and a knifing wind that cut across our ridge and sent sand, dirt, gear, and clothing flying. The morning revealed sandblasted faces and whitened teeth.

We began the day hiking to the west, leaving the trail behind, picking our way over sharp scree boulders, crossing the A. G. Aiken Lava Bed, and moving upward into a giant snowbowl at the foot of Gotchen Glacier. At a scree island in the bowl, we dropped our packs for lunch and a view. Above us, to the east, were towering blue ice cliffs curled over like giant glacial tidal waves, bigger than hospital bills, a reminder that we needed some essential training in this environment. Cecilia was an estimable teacher. We practiced the crucial techniques of self-arrest, using an ice ax to halt a fall; we practiced walking along steep snow slopes; and we reviewed the rules of team survival, including "never step on the rope."

Late afternoon, with a rope assist, we climbed out of the bowl and wound up the steep Suksdorf Ridge, again along a route that seemed untouched by human feet, though a couple of mountain goats mocked our stumblings from a ridge away. Finally, at seven o'clock, near sunset, our guides called camp and we dropped our packs like barbells. The wind sandblasted the camp like a living thing, and at times it seemed we might be picked up and hurled to Oregon. Still, we were alone in our wilderness and, in fact, had not seen another soul beyond our group the entire day. An hour after I pitched my tent, I saw a dim figure struggling up the embankment.

I stepped down the slope and recognized my friend and squash opponent, Jim Laurel, bringing up the rear of our group. His face looked like a gym bag, sweat gleaming on his scalp like Mylar. Examining Jim's fallen shoulders and dull eyes, I knew he wasn't going to make the summit.

At 1:00 A.M. the guides woke us up. It was time. It was just a matter of dressing: two layers of long underwear, pants and top, an expedition suit, a parka, inner and outer gloves, two pairs of wool socks, double-plastic boots, twelve-point steel crampons, gaiters, a helmet, a harness, and a couple of prussic ropes in case we fell into a crevasse and had to climb out. The guides had melted snow the night before, and we filled the water bottles and noshed on bagels while double-checking gear.

We roped into four teams. I was third on our string, led by Cecilia, a link in a four-person chain. As we waded up onto Mazama Glacier, I couldn't help thinking the rope not only protected against falls, but also prevented runaways. The wind was violent in a strobelike way, but the sky was clear.

I had put a set of fresh batteries in my two-inch headlamp the night before, and now I followed the little yellow puddle just ahead of my feet. On my left the mountain loomed, sensed more than seen. Pale snowlight glowed from the empty space below us to the right. The dark mass of the mountain vied with the vacuous space all around us, we few, fragile climbers caught between the two. As the faint glow of the fingernail moon faded, the darkness dissolved. The mountain looked the same in the pale morning light as it had in the pitch of night: angular, distant, coolly impersonal. The sun approached the horizon, and a thick line of neon crimson bled along the edge of the earth. It hung there a long time—it seemed like an hour—before one spot bloomed and the sun rose. In the meantime, distant layers appeared in the rest of the sky, as if glass plates separated the pink morning air on top from the indigo shadows left from night.

We were on the mountain's ice-scoured southern face, and the wind seemed to push the darkness up against our backs. We carried our axes in the hand closest to the mountain, the rope in the other, and awkwardly switched one with the other at the elbow of every switchback. At some point we stopped breaking trail and found a path, a pattern of alternating boot holes in the snow beaten out by climbers who had approached from more popular routes. And then we crossed the tail of our first crevasse, a long gash less than a yard wide at the top but with sculptured blue walls that seemed to cut a bottomless hole into the ice. Stepping by the dark crack, it was easy to envision myself dangling from the end of the tensed nine-millimeter rope—like bait for the catch.

The wind engulfed us. I was sucking the thin atmosphere deeply, expelling it forcefully. We walked in silence, chained souls floating upward together yet alone in our thoughts. As we crested the false summit, my heart sank to see the final steep, 100-meter wall we had yet to ascend to complete our goal. The real summit seemed to roll away as though on wheels. Then we were on a deeply rutted path. My crampon snagged on an edge, and I wrenched my ankle. I grimaced in pain, wishing I could divorce my crampons on grounds of metal cruelty and inadequate means of support.

It seemed like a near-vertical final pitch to the top, and I kicked the front points of my crampons into the snow as Cecilia pulled the rope taut. I couldn't maintain a coil, and the rope went tight as a banjo string. I realized Cecilia was literally pulling us up the mountain. Exhaustion blanketed my thoughts and limbs, and I began to wonder if I had the endurance to make these final meters. I felt like Jim Laurel had looked when he reached camp the night before. I fought for every breath. I was so bone-deep tired, I thought each step might be my last.

Then, almost without warning, we leveled out onto a short path to a snow-covered, collapsed wooden shack. At 9:10 A.M. we stepped up to a shelf and became part of the sky. We were on the 12,000-foot summit, kings of the Cascades, astronauts with the white stuff. Suddenly the simple act of being present assumed a sense of gathered immediacy. The view was too beautiful to behold: to the south, across the Columbia, Oregon's Mount Hood; to the north, Mount Rainier, both floating like islands in a sea of clouds. Atop this Second Mountain, it seemed to be earth's first morning and we the first to bathe in its beauty, unbounded by geography or history. It was a fragment of a cycloramic dream to be on top of this little-known mountain, and I hugged the other team members, just as Tenzing Norgay hugged Ed Hillary on Everest.

And then a stranger summited next to me, flipped open his cell phone, and yelled over the wind into the mouthpiece, "Honey, I'm on top. . . . I feel just like Jon Krakauer."

THE SELWAY

The Selway River, Idaho, U.S.
Running Wolf Creek rapid (class IV), June 2000

THE SELWAY
River of Almost No Return

Cratylus . . . reproached Heraclitus for saying that you cannot step into the same river twice—for he himself thought you could not do so even once.

Aristotle

White-water rafting. Such a tantalizing pairing of words, wet with contour and risk. The *w*'s and the *t*'s slide over and around one another like intertwined snakes, and there are the layers of resonance, managing to evoke temptation and fear at once.

Idaho's Selway is North America's most restricted river, with only sixty-two private rafting permits issued each year and only one group—maximum sixteen participants—allowed to launch per day. The odds of winning the lottery for a permit are about one in thirty. Of the winners, only about 50 percent actually make it on the river, often because the unpredictable water level during the seventy-five-day season is too high or too low. Cited by cognoscenti as the wildest river in the lower forty-eight states, the Selway is also considered one of the toughest, with forty-five named rapids in its forty-seven-mile run, and a reputation for swallowing rafters as though they were pills. Some claim Lord Grizzly still roams here; nobody disputes that the corridor hosts rattlesnakes, wolves, black bears, mountain lions, bighorns, cutthroat trout, black flies, and mosquitoes. Its weather is notorious, with snow and freezing rain possible anytime through June. Even Lewis and Clark were daunted here. When they crossed what is now the Montana–Idaho border in 1805 and considered the cruel country surrounding the Selway, they turned north for Lolo Pass instead.

So it was all the more remarkable that we were halfway down this humming, pine-cloaked river, at the brink of several nasty Class IV rapids. Standing around the campfire sipping bourbon was, among others, the brain trust of the online magazine *Slate:* Michael Kinsley, its editor; Scott Moore, publisher; Scott Shuger, creator and writer of the popular *Slate* section, "Today's Papers"; and Cyrus Krohn, associate publisher. Don't these guys have some sort of key man insurance that requires not traveling together on the same conveyance? Publisher Scott Moore, a plucky outdoorsman who lived in Boise for many years, was the lucky man who drew the Forest Service lottery win for a Selway permit, and who organized this expedition. And he had persuaded several people to join the trip who had never before been rafting, including Michael Kinsley, a man who, though an enthusiastic camper, tells me he simply does not possess the adrenaline gene.

"How did Scott get you on the Selway?" someone asks Michael.

"I thought he said Safeway."

Even I was a tough sell. I had been a professional western river guide for several seasons, and had unsuccessfully entered the Selway lottery half a dozen times, but that was some two decades ago, when in youthful arrogance I refused to be dissuaded by the thought of my own demise. I'd long ago lost the raft in which I ran the Seventies. I wasn't sure I had the pluck and mettle to guide an "expert" river at age forty-nine, especially after spending the last four years rowing a desk at Expedia. I even contacted my friend Snake Hughes, who owns an Idaho rafting outfit, and asked about the launch date Scott was awarded, in late June. His reply: "June 19 can be a stinking high water date, and you do not want to boat the Selway in extreme high flows! The nature of the river is to go from high to low water rapidly in a big flush. Feast/famine. June 19 is a potentially problematic launch date."

Was Scott Moore hauling us to some whitewater-rafting abattoir?

Nonetheless, we gather by the river at a place called Paradise, 3,067 feet above the sea, about eighty miles south of Missoula in the heart of the 1.3 million-acre Selway–Bitterroot Wilderness. The Selway is the sui generis American river, one of the charter designees in the National Wild and Scenic Rivers Act of 1968, and the farthest from any road, concrete, or neon. Here, at the put-in, its currents are a bewildering skein of fluid dynamics. So much water rippling along at different speeds, displaying a glittering richness of surface texture, gives the Selway a parlous, puzzling, vibrant look— the same look I see in my face as I lean over to pull a cooling Icehouse beer from the river.

At 1:12 P.M., our Seattle-based rent-a-guide, Cliff Valentine, smiling like a Grand Inquisitor, calls us all to the river. He has the team put its hands on the neck of a paddle and do a joint locker-room-like crescendoing cheer. It seems half-hearted, but in minutes we launch, the gauge at the Lowell Landing reading three, a thankfully reasonable water level. A year ago on this date the river was in flood, and it would have been suicide to attempt it then.

We have four self-bailing inflatables: one paddle boat, in which all participants wield a paddle in command of a captain, and three oar boats maneuvered by a single guide. There is also a hard-shell kayak, our safety boat, and a couple of self-bailing inflatable kayaks. Because the river has *Giardia lamblia* (the protozoa that causes Beaver Fever), we carry our own water, which is rationed; but we also have sixteen cases of beer. Among the eleven of us, only one has ever seen this river (Scott Moore, who ran it ten years earlier, after the permit season, in very low water), and only two have ever run wild rivers as guides, Cliff and myself. I am concerned with the overall lack of experience, and at the last minute I try to recruit two experts. One declines, but the other, Steve Marks, a Hollywood agent and part-time wild river hound, says yes. But Alaska Airlines delays out of Burbank make it impossible for him to make his connection to Missoula the day of departure, so he will try to hire a private plane to fly him in, and meet us at first night's camp.

So downstream we purl. The river, clear as gin, makes popping sounds, like ice cubes in a drink. The clouds slam shut across the sky, like the door of an observatory dome, and it begins to rain, a cold drizzle. After the first wave everyone is shivering, teeth are chattering.

The day is packed with technical Class II–III rapids (rapids are ranked on a I to VI scale, the latter being a death-trap waterfall). I feel like a character in a Ron Shelton film, an aging athlete finding the zone one last time as I dance the boat through the labyrinthine course. It is great fun, and I am buoyed by this trippy blitz of rapids, and by a sense of collaborating with the forces behind this river wild. But I am also uneasy as I watch the paddleboat, with Michael in it, make crablike runs down straight shots, bumping and slopping, out of control. "Someone on the paddleboat will dump this trip," I tell Scott Shuger, who is riding on my boat. I wince as the paddleboat misses an entry and slews sideways into a rock. We need Steve Marks if the paddleboat is going to make it through the really tough stuff that begins the following day. Even Scott Moore, an active hobbyist rafter, loses his hat and draws blood by scrapping his arm in these first rapids. Jon Nehring, a Montana native and river enthusiast, paddling an inflatable kayak, twice pops out into the river.

Scott Shuger is now shivering mightily, and so for distraction, we take to talking movies—manufactured realities usually coveted for offering more adventure than real life; but here, the celluloid editions serve the opposite, and seem respites from the harshness of the Selway.

Late in the afternoon we pull into camp at Shearer, where Steve is supposed to meet us, but he's not here. I hike to the overgrown airfield, stepping over bear scat, and trek downriver about a mile, hoping Steve might be somewhere here, but there is no sign of him.

Back at camp, Michael fiddles with his GPS and determines that we are right where the map says we are; spatula jockey Dave Wood (one of two of Scott Moore's uncles on the trip), along with Cliff, cooks up a storm—mussels, baby back ribs, and Albertson's potatoes au gratin—complemented by a bottle of Marilyn Merlot; someone shows up with a handful of ripe huckleberries, and a lively horseshoe game is tossed. All with an ear to the sky, hoping at the last minute Steve Marks will arrive. But finally the shutter of darkness closes, and hope is gone. I stumble to bed, and see that a roll of toilet paper I had left by the side of the tent has been chewed to shreds by some animal. I zip up the tent and slip to sleep.

I awake with the sound of a mosquito buzzing my ear and slap at it, but the sound only gets louder. Then I realize it's a plane, a plane, and bust out of the tent and run to the airfield. Sure enough, a four-seater Cessna 172 drops out of the sky and bounces along the grassy strip. Out steps Steve, dressed in black fleece, looking like Harvey Keitel's Vincent the Cleaner, or his Winston Wolf, here to make things right.

After a buttermilk pancake and rasher of bacon breakfast and a wallop of Starbucks, we load the boats and roll downstream. Scott Shuger, hearing that paddling keeps the body warmer than riding in the oar boat, trades with Michael, who now rides with me.

Overhead four hawks ride the eddies of the wind; an osprey dives, surfacing with a fish. A hermit thrush calls from the shade of an ancient cedar tree, and a gaggle of red-breasted mergansers paddles around an eddy. We pull into a beach rimmed with arrowleaf balsamroot, across from the Selway Lodge, first homesteaded in 1898 and now the only lived-in structure on this stretch of river. My friend Tom Peirce and his family owned and operated the lodge for many years, and when they put it up for sale in the early 1990s,

I fancied buying it, but couldn't afford it. Now it is someone else's own private Idaho. A log bridge spans the river, and Scott Moore promptly struts to its middle, strips off his shirt, and jumps in. The man has balsamroots. If Michelin awarded stars for fearlessness, Scott Moore would collect three of them.

Not far downstream we approach our first Class IV rapid of the trip, Ham. Already, Steve has whipped his paddle crew into shape, and they're ready for the test.

The central feature of Ham is a giant rock in the middle of the river with a surface smooth as monument stone. The main current shatters against its middle and does a roiling bop down the sides. Scott says he wants to follow my run, so as I launch he pushes out as well, a few yards behind. I popple down the right side, a clean run, but then look back to watch Scott's run, and he's not there. We wait an interminable time and then see Scott come caroming through with one oar bent in the middle like a bird's wing. Turns out Scott had turned to watch the boat upstream, and had crashed into a rock above Ham, smashing his oar. He made it to shore, where he switched with his spare oar and made a decent run through Ham. Steve and Cliff make the run as though whistling through a rifle barrel.

Though we have much to celebrate with our successful runs today, the evening is a somber one as we ponder what's ahead. We're camped just above Moose Creek, a tributary that disembogues enough to nearly double the volume of the Selway. For most of its course the Selway drops an average of twenty-eight feet per mile, more than triple the gradient of the Colorado River as it runs through the Grand Canyon. But the section just downstream jumps off a bridge, falling 150 feet and tearing through ten rapids in just three miles. It's this stretch where the eschatologists, those philosophers who study the human soul and its relation to judgment and death, ponder our attraction to the flame of risk: Most of the Selway's drownings occur in this stretch of water.

A few of us hike downstream to view the hydrotechnics, and even from the path a hundred feet above the river we can see the grotesque mushroom boils, the sharp falls, the keeper holes. The river seems to go insane, liquid chaos frothing, twisting, skibbling around and doubling back on itself like rogue fireworks. We can hear the rapids' thunder pealing through the burled gorge. We spend the waning light scouting the cataracts, trying to pick out routes, and I'm seized with a feeling of horripilation: Things could go very wrong tomorrow. Back at camp, conversation and dinner are spare; spaghetti, halibut, and wine in a box. Dyspepsia hangs in the air. Everyone heads to bed early; Steve Marks takes a Valium.

At breakfast, as the peaks unravel themselves from the morning fog, Michael announces he will take the Forest Service trail around the big rapids today, rendezvousing with us at Meeker Creek, five miles downstream. He wants to experience a little wilderness solitude, and doesn't get a thrill from riding close to the edge in big white water. It seems a smart idea, and I am a bit envious, knowing I can't take this option, as I have to row one of the rafts. And now I will row it without a passenger, which is a loss of needed ballast and bowline handling.

After Michael takes off, someone wonders aloud: "Will Michael be safe from the wildlife trekking alone?"

"Are you kidding?" Cyrus rejoins, "With the Northwest Kinsley's razor-sharp wit, I fear for the animals."

It's a perfect day to get wet, sunny and cloudless. Cliff has us perform another group whoop, and suggests another river ritual, whereby we scoop up a handful of the giardia-laden water and swoosh it around the inside of our mouths, asking for favor from the river gods; then we spit it back to the river. Never superstitious, I do the ritual regardless. Scott Moore does not. By eleven o'clock we're off into the rapids. Scott gets swept into Double Dip without scouting, and comes close to the tipping point, washing through, emerging to the eddy looking like a crustacean with its shell off.

We come to Ladle, considered the toughest rapid on the river, and make a long scout. There is no logic to Ladle; the river takes sudden tours around rocks, splits off in two or three erratic directions at once, then convenes again, as though in a square dance of the mad. On the far right there seems a passage, but then I see that spars of fallen fir bristle at the final drop like a cheval-de-frise. Only through close study can I see if a route will play, or veer off into an illusion, or a rock, or worse, into the craterlike fissure of a souse hole with its twisted, churning mouth waiting for a catch. I'm tempted to plot my course on paper, analyzing the hydraulics, factoring the weight distribution on my boat. But anatomizing rapids is like translating a poem; it risks missing the unanalyzable spirit of the thing, its beautiful and hazardous play upon freedom. I finally just walk back upstream, tug my lifejacket tight, and head into the maelstrom, where I make a pretty run. Jack Visco, who is paddling the safety kayak, decides to portage halfway down the rapid. Steve, whose crack crew is not quite ready for Olympic competition, makes a rowdy run, hanging up for long minutes on a rock midstream toward the end. Cliff ricochets down the course like a pinball. Scott, going last, though, slams into the wall at the end, and almost flips again. He shouldn't have ignored Cliff's ritual.

Downstream I sweep by an overhanging branch, and a grist of bees buzzes out. Two sting me on the back of the neck as I'm entering Little Niagara rapids, and it feels like someone has applied a poultice of broken glass above my shoulders, but I grit my teeth, keep my focus, and make the run with the flare of a figure skater, as well as subsequent runs down Puzzle Creek, No Slouch, Halfway Creek, and Miranda Jane. And, when we pull in at the appointed tributary creek on the right bank (where else?) to pick up Michael, the beach is crowded with butterflies. Michael saunters down to the river's edge and mock scowls, "I called for this taxi two hours ago."

Later, though, as we nosh on peanut butter sandwiches and watch a deer swim across the river, Michael shares his psychic valence: "That was the most beautiful hike I have ever done. I'm very glad, though, I was up on the path, and you were down there."

As we pull into camp, a snake slithers out of the root around which I tie the bowline. But fear is history now, so I ignore the snake and go about business, setting up camp, bathing in the cold river, uncorking bottles. In the furbelows and folderol of the chat between the first swig of Chilean pisco and the puff of a Cuban cigar, Doug and Dave Wood walk down the beach wearing specially made "Department of Justice, Anti-Trust Division" black tee shirts, and Michael plays taps on a kazoo. The worst is behind us, and we celebrate deep into the night.

"I know I had a good night when I wake up with my sunglasses on," Cliff greets the group the last morning. The sky squeezes the lemons of dawn, and I slip on my wet-suit booties and start doing a barmy hop, as some stinging bug is at my heel.

Finally we're on the last few miles of river. There is one last Class IV rapid, Wolf Creek, and Michael chooses to walk around, even though there is no path so it requires some aggressive bouldering and bushwhacking through vegetation with claws. The run has two routes; the right is a relatively easy straight line that ends in a piling wave. Steve, Scott, and Cliff all make fine runs. I eye the left side, a serpentine set of maneuvers around a series of exposed rocks, stepping down toward a funnel that disappears between two boulders that turn the air between them white. The worst obstacle is a rock shaped like a peacock tail near the end of the rapid, where a current hoses into it then plumes out like a parachute. A missed stroke would almost certainly spell trouble. But I've been dancing my whole way down the river, stitching the current like a needleman. I decide to go for it. I'm performing every bit as well as when I was half my age, and the past now seems authentic, achievable, like a fish shimmering beneath the surface of shallow water.

Overflowing with hubris, I pitch the boat toward Wolf Creek Rapids. The entry is perfect, and I make the tight pull past the first boulder and glissade through the top parts of the rapids. But, as any movie-goer knows, this is a ritual scene rich in peripety; it is always the cop about to retire, the thief out for one more score, the lover promising the adventure will be his last, the guide running the final big rapid, who has the fatal reversal of fortune. For an instant, heady with my success, I let my guard down, and suddenly I slam into the rock, the rock radiating water like a fan. I hit it square, and the raft thrumms as though it were a tree struck by an axe. Then the boat buckles in half, yanking my right oar from my grip, and rears as if bent on catapulting me into the roiling soup. Suddenly a deep silence sweeps in and hovers around for an endless second. I seem stuck in a horologic hole. Then the sound pours in again, as into a bowl, and the buzz of the river's prop slices through me ear to ear. Against the river's will, I manage to hang on. I snatch the flying oar from the air and push its throat back into its lock as the boat skids, out of control, on a crackling surge of foam through the last part of the rapid. At the egress, I spin the raft around and miraculously land at the beach at Michael Kinsley's waiting feet. "I was almost up the creek without a paddler," he chides as he crawls into my boat, knowing well there are no more big rapids downstream.

There is only one more moment of terror—when I mistakenly inform Scott Moore there are only twenty cans of beer left. His jaw drops, his face whitens like a balloon about to burst, and he looks more frightened than at any of the rapids. Ooops . . . my mistake, I correct, as I open a cooler on my boat and find at least 100 more cans.

The last miles of the day are relatively smooth, and Michael asks to take over the oars. He's quite good, and with some pointers, he makes good runs down some Class II rapids. He could be a guide someday.

The paddleboat sneaks up on us as Michael is making some final strokes, and its occupants break out into a chorus, "Michael row your boat ashore."

"Not like I never heard that in summer camp," he grins. And he steers the raft to the take-out.

ESCAPE TO BORNEO

ESCAPE TO BORNEO

The world is nothing but the sacred land, and the sacred land is inhabited only by the sacred people.

From the tradition of the Dayak of Borneo

One of the world's great city views is from Kowloon, looking across the Victoria Harbor to the mountainous concrete, glass, and steel spires on the island of Hong Kong. From Hong Kong looking back, the views were never so lofty, because for seventy-three years the low-flying planes of nearby Kai Tak Airport required building height restrictions. Now, though, with the 1998 opening of the new Hong Kong International Airport at Chek Lap Kok, some powerful unleashed energy is pushing the Kowloon landscape higher, like a time-lapse crashing of tectonic plates forever lifting great mountain ranges farther above the clouds.

Recently after giving a talk at a conference in Hong Kong, I spent some time resting in my room on the forty-first floor of the Renaissance Harbour View Hotel, gazing at the mountains-in-the-making across the way in Kowloon, and wondered how close might I find the real thing. An unfurl of the map showed that the highest mountain between the Himalayas and New Guinea was Mount Kinabalu at 13,455 feet, in the Malaysian state of Sabah on the island of Borneo, just three hours' flight to the southeast. Climbing a mountain without an elevator was strictly against doctor's orders, as two weeks earlier I had undergone surgery for an inguinal hernia repair and was told to lay low. But in researching Mount Kinabalu, I discovered the summit was called Low's Peak, after Hugh Low, the European who first climbed the mountain in the middle nineteenth century. That seemed to signal some sort of terranean permission to sally forth, my handicap notwithstanding.

The weekend was nigh, so the following morning I was on an MAS flight to the state capital of Kota Kinabalu, just four degrees north of the equator, for a potentially gut-wrenching, four-day adventure in the Malaysian Borneo state of Sabah.

For more than a century, since explorers and missionaries first ventured into the interior of Borneo, outsiders have been captivated by its half-truths and half-fictions, awed by its headhunting heritage, its tales of giant insects and snakes, of wild men who lived in trees, of prodigious leeches that stood up when sensing a human. Borneo, dominated by millions of acres of tropical rain forests on the world's third largest island, was the stuff of nightmares.

The name *Sabah* means "Land Below the Wind," a place where early maritime traders sought refuge beneath the typhoon belt of the Philippines. This northeastern quadrant of the island once was overlorded by an Englishman, the publisher Alfred Dent, who leased it from the Sultan of Sulu for five thousand dollars a year and called it British North Borneo. It was State administered as a business venture until 1942, when the Japanese invaded and took control. After the Second World War, the British returned and Borneo became a crown colony. In 1963, Sabah gained independence and joined the Federation of Malaysia.

From the Kota Kinabalu airport I stepped into the Borneo night. The air was saturated and hot, with a slightly sweet odor. Even though it was dark, I could sense the mountain to the east, bending me with its silent mind. Mount Kinabalu is the most accessible big mountain in the tropics, with direct road access to the mountain's trailhead. I rode the sixty miles from the coast up to the eponymous park headquarters, where I had dinner and checked into a spacious split-level chalet that a concessionaire had built for use by climbers. This was base camp with style.

As I sipped port on the balcony, tiny life in the tropical tangle a few yards away broadcast news of my presence in a steady din of clicks, trills, buzzes, and other noises that ranged from the sound of deep-fat frying to the shrieking of car alarms. But there was more than strident bugs in this backcloth of biodiversity beyond my feet. The 300-square-mile national park's famous flora includes more than 1,000 orchid species, 450 ferns, 40 kinds of oak, 27 rhododendrons, and the world's largest flower, the rafflesia, whose stem bears platter-size flowers. In all, Mount Kinabalu's ecosystem, which is about the same size as that of Mount Rainer in Washington State, is home to 4,000 to 4,500 vascular plant species, more than a quarter the number of all recorded species in the United States.

The next morning I stepped onto the porch and over a moth the size of a bat, then outside into a day tidy and bright. For the first time I could see the striking granite massif, which looks like a mad ship riding high rain forest waves, with fantastic masts, tines, spires, and aiguilles dotted across its pitched and washed deck of rock at over 13,000 feet. It had rained all night and, as a result, waterfalls spilled down the mountain's sides as though a tide had just pulled back from a cliff.

Borneo was formed as a result of plate movements that united two separate portions of the island some fifty million years ago. Mount Kinabalu lies near the site where the two parts joined at the north-eastern tip of the island. About forty million years ago, the region lay under the sea and accumulated thick layers of marine sediments, creating sandstone and shale, which later uplifted to form the Crocker Range. Mount Kinabalu started out about 10 million years ago as a huge ball of molten granite, called a "pluton," lying beneath the sedimentary rocks of the Crocker Range. This pluton slowly cooled between 9 and 4 million years ago, and about a million years ago it was thrust from the bowels of the earth and grew to a height probably several thousand feet higher than it is today. When the Pleistocene Ice Age emerged, rivers of ice covered Kinabalu, eventually wearing down the soft sandstone and shale and shrinking the summit. Low's Peak, the highest point on Kinabalu, and the horned towers of the mountain were created by the bulldozing of these huge glaciers. The youngest nonvolcanic mountain in the world, Kinabalu is still growing, the living tension of colliding plates pushing upward at the rate of a quarter of an inch a year.

Checking in at the Registration Office at Park Headquarters, I saw a sign that said nobody could climb to the summit without hiring a certified guide. So I enlisted Eric Ebid, thirty, a mild man of Borneo, small, enthusiastic, with bad teeth but a ready and real smile, and eyes the color of wet coal that looked as though they could see every forest twitch. He spoke little English but had a knack for communicating and a beautiful singing voice. His shoes were made of thin rubber and were not much more than sandals, but he walked with a spring that made his limbs appear to be made from resilient saplings. When he shook hands, he first touched his hand to his heart and bowed, a local greeting used among friends. Eric was a Dusun, the dominant ethnic group of northern Borneo. The Dusuns have lived on the flanks of Mount Kinabalu for centuries and believe that the spirits of their ancestors reside on the summit, the realm of the dead. They call the mountain Aki Nabula, "Revered Place of the Dead." The Dusuns were once warlike and used to carry their captives in bamboo cages up the slopes of the mountain, then spear them to death in the shadow of its jagged summit. But the current generation of Kinabalu Dusuns has given up the spear for the walking stick, and war cries for hiking songs.

The park bus labored to get to the trailhead two and a half zigzagging miles up the hill, at a power station at 6,100 feet that not only supplies electricity to Kota Kinabalu but has a cable that stretches up the mountain to supply a rest house two miles above sea level.

Off the bus, I stepped through a gate into a world steaming and flourishing, rife with birdsong. I was in the last place on Earth for many of the world's rarest plants and wildlife, an ancient dipterocarp rain forest, far older than the arbors of the Amazon Basin.

The ascent began with a descent, losing 100 feet of altitude and dropping us into a rain forest as lush and improbable as the canvases of Henri Rousseau. Then, in earnest, we began the unrelenting five-mile rise, switching back and forth over razorbacked ridges, through groves of broad-leaved oak, laurel, and chestnut that were draped in mosses, epiphytes, and liverworts and thickened with a trumpeting of ferns. The trail was fashioned of tree limbs pinioned to serve as risers and occasionally as posts and handrails, a stairway pulled directly from nature. At much-appreciated regular intervals, there were charming gazebos with toilets and tanked water. I stopped at the first, refilling my water bottle.

For a million years Kinabalu was a place where only imaginations and spirits traveled; no one disturbed the dead there—until the British arrived. In 1851 Sir Hugh Low, a British colonial secretary, bushwhacked to the first recorded ascent, accompanied by local tribal guides and their chief, who purified the trespass by sacrificing a chicken and seven eggs. They also left a cairn of charms along the way, including human teeth. Not to be outdone, Sir Hugh left a bottle with a note recording his feat, which he later characterized as "the most tiresome walk I have ever experienced."

By late morning we entered the cloud forest, where the higher altitude and thinner soil begin to twist and warp the vegetation. There were constant pockets and scarves of fog. At 7,300 feet we passed through a narrow-leafed forest where Miss Gibbs' Bamboo climbed into the tree trunks, clinging to limbs like a delicate moss. Lillian Gibbs, an English botanist and the first woman known to scale Mount Kinabalu, collected more than a thousand botanical specimens here for the British Museum in 1910, at a time when there were no rest houses, shelters, or corduroyed trails.

By midday the weather had turned grim; skies opened, the views down the mountain were blotted, and the climb was more like an upward wade through a thick orange soup of alkaline mud. I was soaked to the skin, but the rain was warm, as if it was all meant to be humane, even medicinal. For a moment, I forgot my hernia.

Still, when the rain became a deluge, we stopped at the Layang Layang Staff Headquarters (which was locked shut) for a rest, hoping that the downpour might subside. We were at 8,600 feet, better than halfway to our sleeping hut. While there, we munched on cheese sandwiches and hard-boiled eggs, sipped bottled water. I watched as a small parade of tiny women, bent beneath *burongs* (elongated cane baskets) heaped high above their heads with loads of food, fuel, and beer for the overnight hut, marched by on sure feet, trekking to serve the tourists who flock to this mountain.

The first tourist made the climb in 1910, and, in the same year, so did the first dog, a bull terrier named Wigson. Since the paving of the highway from Kota Kinabalu in 1982, tourist development has been rapid, by Borneo's standards. More than twenty thousand people a year now reach Low's Peak—the highest point—via the Paka Spur route, the one we were ascending, and hundreds of Dusuns are employed in getting outsiders up and down and around the mountain trails.

After thirty minutes the rain hurtled even harder, so we shrugged and continued upward into the heart of the cloud forest, among groves of knotted and gnarled tea-trees, whose lichen-encrusted trunks and limbs were stunted and twisted like overgrown bonsai. We stepped over foot-long purple worms, black and brown frogs, and a black beetle the size of an ice ax.

As we climbed, Eric sang songs in a voice as sweet as papaya. Between tunes he pointed out various rhododendrons, with blooms that ranged from peach to pink, and the insectivorous pitcher plants, whose pods were the size of avocadoes. Instead of nutrients in the soil, they feed on trapped insects. Coming out of a long leaf was the trapping mechanism, a tendril and cup with a mouth that looked like a tiny steam shovel, or the lead in the movie *Little Shop of Horrors*. Local lore has it that Spenser St. John, a botanist who climbed Kinabalu with Hugh Low on his second expedition in 1862, found a pitcher plant containing a drowned rat floating in six pints of water.

At 9,000 feet the terrain began to change drastically. Here an outcropping of ultramafic rock made for an orange, toxic soil, out of which struggled a forest of dwarf pine and myrtle. It was here that I met an Australian on his way down. Though young and hulkish, he looked, in a word, awful—dour and green—and was of the ancient mariner sort, shaken and full of foreboding advice. "You should only do this, mate, if you are in great, great shape," he said, and I felt a ping where my hernia scar pinched.

Accustomed to the Spartan A-frames and Quonsets that serve as huts on other mountains I have climbed, I was unprepared for the majesty of the spruce-wood Laban Rata Guesthouse. Anchored on stilts at the edge of a cliff just above 11,000 feet, two stories tall with a happy yellow roof, the place was like a boutique hotel. Its cozy lounge featured a decorative Christmas tree and a set of Christmas cards, even though this was May, and a television with a satellite feed showing The Travel Channel. On one wall, certificates stating summit success were prematurely for sale. Plate-glass windows allowed views down the mountain, where we watched clouds stream through crags and treetops like rivers of fine chalk. When the rain stopped, I stepped outside and watched the clouds blow off the mountain above, and suddenly there was an empire of silvery gray granite, castled with barren crags, as awesome as the slopes of Rundle Mountain in Banff or Half Dome in Yosemite, thick rivulets of water shaving off the smooth face in falls.

The canteen menu ranged from fresh fish to fried rice to french fries and Guinness. In my room, which slept four, there was an electric light and a small electric heater that allowed me to dry my clothes, and down the hall were hot showers.

Exhausted from the day's trek, I fell into the arms of Morpheus around seven, trusting that Eric would come by with a wake-up knock around 3:00 A.M. The motivation for starting in the wee hours was that tropical mountains typically cloud over after sunrise, and often it begins to rain soon after, making an ascent at a reasonable hour not only more difficult but dangerous, and the coveted views nonexistent.

Sure enough, at the crack of three there was a knock on the door. One of my roommates, a British woman who was suffering a headache, announced she would not be going farther. Another half-dozen at the hut would also turn around here, suffering from exhaustion or altitude sickness. I felt sorry for them, but I also felt proud of myself that, despite my wound, I had the moxie and strength to continue. I fumbled for my hiking boots and tripped downstairs for a cup of tea. At 3:20 I donned my headlamp and set out under a blue-black sky hung with a glittering Milky Way. The stars seemed as near and thick as when I was a child. I listened for ghosts, but everything was bone quiet and cool. This was truly a mountain of the dead.

I followed the little white pool of light my headlamp cast on the granite just ahead of my feet. Looking back, I saw a constellation of twenty or so headlamp beams bobbing and flashing as their owners negotiated in my footsteps. I was amazed that in my condition I could be ahead of so many.

The emergence at tree line onto the cold granite face was abrupt, just as the first gold and pink bands of dawn cracked open and singed the sky. It was like stepping from a closet into a ballroom, and everyone seemed to move a little faster, enamored by the tap against their boots of unwrapped stone, rhyming with the rock. *"Pelan, pelan,"* (slowly, slowly) advised Eric, as though he knew of my injury. As my guide, Eric had been practically tethered to me throughout, never more than a few steps away. His pace was thankfully deliberate, allowing time to stop and observe and admire the grand views and the tiny miracles of nature. Other guides were out front, herding their clients as though on a chase. But Eric took his time, his wide eyes ever searching for some piece of magic to share, his feet moving to the tempo of his soulful ballads.

At places where the rock angled up forty degrees or more, solicitous trail builders had anchored expansion bolts and fixed stout, white ropes. At one point, at the rock face of Panar Laban (Place of Sacrifice), where early guides stopped to appease the souls of their ancestors, we got down on our knees and scrambled upward on all fours.

In the robed light of 6:00 A.M., clambering up an aplite dike, a vertical mass of igneous rock that has forced its way upward through overlying strata, I could make out the pinnacles surrounding us, legacies of the Ice Age: the Ugly Sisters and malformed Donkey's Ears on our right, immense St. John's and South Peak on our left. Low's Peak was tucked in between, like a storm-tossed ship caught between frozen waves. The smooth plates we had been scaling became a pile of frost-shattered blocks and boulders, forming a jumble of giant tesserae in search of a mosaic.

To the roof of Borneo we scrabbled, just as *mata hari* (sun, in Malay) showed its face. I sucked some thin air and looked around. It was stunning to watch the mountaintop as it was transfigured by sunrise. The undulant granite towers warmed with sunlight as guides lit up their cigarettes. It seemed like the Tower of Babel as each new climber made the last step and cheered in German, Japanese, Australian, or Bahasa. I basked now in the bliss of standing bare against the heavens, with the fathomless interior of Borneo far below me. On one side fell the mile-deep ravine that is Low's Gully, sometimes called Death Valley or Place of the Dead, believed to be guarded by a slaying dragon, where in 1994 a British Army expedition got famously stuck in the jungle-filled slash. Padi fields, *kampungs* (villages), and an endless expanse of jungle unfolded on another side; the dancing lights of Kota Kinabalu and the shimmering South China Sea appeared on a third side.

I circled the broken bottleneck of Low's Peak, taking in each facet. When I completed the circle and looked west again, sunrise hard on my back, the immense shadow of Kinabalu, a huge, dark-blue cone, seemed to fly over the land and sea, stretching to the horizon. It was sublime; there was nothing to improve this moment and place.

I reached down and felt the scar from my recent operation. I felt light-headed, filled to the brim with the helium of gratefulness, and felt pretty trick that I had done what my doctor had said I should not. I felt glued together with sweat and brio, king of the jungle, and strutted and posed. Until I looked across the plateau and saw a tall, dark-haired woman limping toward me, balanced by a pair of ski poles.

She sat down near me and pulled up her pants leg to reveal a full brace that went from her lower leg to her thigh. "What happened?" I couldn't help but ask, and in a Dutch accent she replied, "Skiing accident in the Alps a couple weeks ago. Destroyed my ACL—that's my anterior cruciate ligament. Doctor said I couldn't climb mountains for six months. But I couldn't resist, so here I am."

Her words and deed humbled me. After all, adventure is a relative quest, and for every person who has summited Everest as a personal best, there is someone, perhaps handicapped, who pushed even harder to climb a neighboring hill, or complete a first lowland hike. Happy for the success of the Dutch woman, and rightly effaced, I started back down the mountain.

Back in Hong Kong once again, I stayed at the Regent Hotel, closest hotel to the waterfront, with the finest view of the Hong Kong Island skyline. As I sat back in the hotel Jacuzzi nursing my wounds with a gin and tonic, gazing at the simulacra mountains, the evening light dashed off the windowed pinnacles and spires, piercing a sea of clouds. Here, if I squinted, the illusion was complete, and I could overlay the crowns of Kinabalu with those of the former crown colony. Mountains, I realized, be they made by man or nature, reconciled the bourgeois love of order with the bohemian love of emancipation. However handicapped, some people belong in those high palaces, and I was one of them.

THE FIRST KIVA

THE GRAND CANYON, ARIZONA, U.S.
*Mesas and creosote bushes cover the Womb of the World, as the
Hopi refer to Mother Earth.*

THE FIRST KIVA

That she belov'd knows nought that knows not this:
Men prize the thing ungain'd more than it is.
William Shakespeare
Troilus and Cressida, Act 1, Scene 2

Some say it is the most sacred site in America, and it is a secret to all but a few. It exists on no maps, no brochures, not even a website. There are no guidebooks that tell how to find it. In fact, it is forbidden to visit if you are not of the tribe.

The place is Sipapu, and it is a travertine dome concealed somewhere in a tributary corridor of the Grand Canyon. The explorer John Wesley Powell suggested it could be the legendary fountain of youth. The Hopi believe it is the center of the cosmos, the umbilical cord leading from somewhere in the innermost chambers of Mother Earth to the heavens, and the place of mankind's emergence from the underworld. There is no place more sacred to the Hopi, the oldest carriers of ancient Indian beliefs and practices.

The ten thousand Hopi, who live in the arid highlands of northern Arizona, have inhabited the same place for a millennium, far longer than any other people in North America. They are not only the oldest dwellers in this land but are considered by some who have studied them to have a wisdom, a knowledge of things, beyond average comprehension. Peace-loving and knit tightly together by clan relationships, they are intensely spiritual and fiercely independent. Their religion, deep and all-pervading, is a many-stranded cord that unites them to their stark and beautiful environment. Sipapu is their tabernacle and their secret.

A quarter-century ago I was an untutored river guide on the Colorado River, which winds through the Grand Canyon. On most trips we would stop for a snack and a swim at a major south-side tributary that ran with the blue-green brilliance of Navajo jewelry on a bolo tie. On one such break as we packed up the remains of lunch, the senior guide told me about Sipapu, describing a twenty-foot-high carbonate cupola about five miles up the tributary canyon. There was a pit in the center of the dome that bubbled with pale green water. According to legend, the water served as a lid, so that ordinary humans could not see the magical things going on beneath the surface. He said the Hopi believed that beneath the pit was the end of a rainbow. It was a bridge to the gateway to this world, the Fourth World, *Tuwaqachi,* World Complete, from the pre-emergence place.

Though he had never seen it, he knew of another guide who had. Soon after his visit to Sipapu, the guide was piloting his raft through one of the biggest rapids of the Colorado, Lava Falls, and capsized, something to be avoided at all costs in this horrible maelstrom. The other guides on the trip speculated about a connection between his unsanctioned visit and the flip. Whatever the reason, divine intervention or not, the guide quit the river and was never seen in the Grand Canyon again.

For seven seasons I rafted the Colorado, and each time I passed the azure tributary, which I learned the Hopi called *Paayu,* I wondered about making a pilgrimage hike. And then, remembering what happened to the guide who had made the visit, I thought better of it.

Now, with a ripened perspective, I decided I would at last make the journey. I was no longer a young river guide fearing capsizes or river retribution; since then I had spent years stealing across international borders in search of adventure and stories and had long ago twisted the word "forbidden" to mean "invitation." There is little left on the planet that has not been abundantly examined by some interested party, be it an explorer, a scientist, or a developer. I imagined hiking into this hidden place and photographing, recording, videotaping, and writing about Sipapu, staging a kind of journalistic coup. *National Geographic* had been pulling back the lids of the unknown and sacrosanct for more than 100 years, often justifying the act by suggesting that, in revealing and revering sacred places to a mass audience, an interested constituency would be created that could come to their aid if such sites were threatened by more nefarious plans. I believed in that. But, at the same time, over the years since my Grand Canyon guiding days, I had come to believe that the idea of the sacred was quite simply one of the most conservative notions in any culture, because it seeks to turn other ideas—uncertainty, progress, change—into crimes. And to that I did not aspire.

But there was trouble from the outset. I well knew the Hopi had withstood the unraveling effect of white man's society more successfully than any other Native American culture, and that their mytho-religious ceremonies were often off-limits to outsiders. But back when I was a guide, the Hopis were conducting bus tours through their reservation and seemed keen to earn money through tourism. Hoping the allure of touro-dollars would entice the Hopi to allow a journalistic showcase of Sipapu, I called the Hopi Cultural Preservation Office in Kykotsmovi, Arizona, and asked for a guide and interpreter. The rebuff rumbled through the phone. Nobody would guide me; nobody would speak to me; I would not be allowed to see it. There would be no photographs. They didn't care about tourism potential. Stay away, was the resounding message.

That just fueled my resolve. Almost like a child who becomes more determined as the parent says no, I became more focused on the job. I called Tom, an old friend and fellow ex-guide, in Flagstaff. He and his wife had hiked down the Hopi Salt Trail from the Canyon rim to Sipapu twenty years ago with an idea to offer tours, but when they got back from the outing their marriage fell apart, and he never went back. But he did have his map and some crude directions he would loan me.

So I teamed up with an ace multi-media producer who would capture video, stills, and sounds of the site while I would write. We would present Sipapu on the Internet in all of its colors, hums, and facets, a virtual display, the closest thing to guiding the audience itself to the site.

Then, after weeks of planning, on the morning of departure my multi-media guy cancelled, recruited to go to St. Louis and cover Mark McGwire's attempt to break the single-season home run record. Undaunted, I grabbed my trusty camera and headed to the airport. At least there would be images and words.

In Flagstaff Tom gave me background on the ancient Hopi Salt Trail, the path from the Grand Canyon rim to Sipapu, and beyond it to a series of natural sodium chloride seeps. Since prehistoric times, people made the precarious journey to the salt mines near the sacred site, returning with the precious crystals to be used in sacred ceremonies. Today, since salt is readily available at the trading post or convenience store, it is rare for a Hopi to make the journey, and few others had ever found the way down the trail.

After buying fresh film and supplies, I headed north to the Hopi reservation. I hoped by meeting in person some of the key tribal members they might reconsider my proposition. Driving north up Route 87 from Winslow, I entered the 4,000-square-mile Hopi Reservation. Flat-topped red and brown mesas loomed, and overhead a few plum-colored clouds followed as though they were Kachinas, the revered spirits of ancestors and creation, and the carriers of rain, watching my journey. I drove up to Second Mesa and stopped at the first curio shop to ask directions. I asked the shopkeeper if she knew anything about Sipapu. With the darting, lateral eyes of a hunted species, she said no and vanished into the back room.

A few miles down the road I came to the Hopi Cultural Center, a flat-roofed sprawl of mortared sandstone. Inside I introduced myself and asked if anyone might be around who could help with my proposed journey. Everyone who might help was away, I was told by the receptionist. She didn't suggest I return later.

I wandered into the Hopi Heritage Museum, attached to the Cultural Center, and asked the curator about Sipapu, but he claimed ignorance, and instead tried to sell me a picture book. I had lunch at the adjacent restaurant, where the young Hopi waitress seated me in the only booth with broken lights, though the place was empty. After ordering the *piiki* (Hopi blue-corn flour bread) and *noqkwiwi* (a traditional lamb and corn stew), I asked her what she knew of Sipapu. Her dark marble eyes locked into mine as she told me the young people didn't really know about the ancient ways, and then she turned away.

It was getting late, and I hoped to get to the trailhead by dark, so I drove east across a bleak terrain of crumbling yellow sandstone, shored up by shiplike geological remains, flat topped and forbidding. I crossed the Navajo Reservation, then went through Tuba City, across the Painted Desert, and up to The Gap, named for a huge break in the Echo Cliffs overlooking Route 89. The cliffs had the appearance of a muddy sea frozen in the midst of a storm. The setting seemed to be from an old Western film, and in fact it was: *The Last Frontier* and Zane Grey's *Heritage of the Desert* were filmed here.

According to Tom's map, The Gap was just a mile from the turn-off toward the trailhead. I filled up at the gas station and asked the Navajo attendant what he knew of Sipapu. His deeply etched face gave me a puzzled look and said, "Never heard of it."

"But that's impossible. The turn-off is just a mile from your gas station."

He just spun his back to me and went about his business.

I walked across the street to The Gap Trading Post and bought final supplies for the hike, including two gallon-jugs of water. At the register I asked the attendant if she knew about Sipapu. She shook her head no and gave me a cryptic smile, looking very much like a bemused Marilyn Whirlwind from "Northern Exposure." I asked again, prodded by her smile, and she said, "Well, I have driven to the trailhead; it's a long ways. You should be careful. Do you have raingear?" When I said no, she offered me a garbage bag to use as a poncho, and as I left I saw her spectral face floating like a lantern in the dark room.

A mile up the road I turned west, off the road, into the vast tan desert of the Coconino Plateau. The sky was darkening, and a couple of satiny-black ravens flew in front of my windshield, looking like Hopi thunderbirds. I followed Tom's directions—left at the stone hogan, right at the corral, follow the dry washbed, straight past the red sandstone cairn—but I quickly got lost. I was stuck in a labyrinth, a latticework of dirt roads that scratched across the desert like claw marks on the back of the land. I wrestled the wheel of the Ford Explorer like a captain in a typhoon. There was nothing logical about these roads. They took sudden detours around rocks, split off in two or three erratic directions at once, then convened again like desert rivulets in a thunderstorm. Often only a tremor of instinct told me whether I was still following the track or had veered off into a mirage, or worse, toward one of the craterlike fissures caused by erosion that look like the open mouths of crocodiles, waiting for an errant fish.

I wandered for two hours, utterly lost, and when night pitched its tent, I pitched my own in a *cabine de lux,* a roofless abandoned stone hogan on a hill, above any flash-flood paths. It stormed all night, ceaseless buckets of rain with no mercy unlike any I had seen in my years of guiding. Rain is scarce here and therefore is a driving force of the Hopi religion. When rain comes their prayers are answered. Forks of lightning like illuminated nerves and thunder like gunfire tore apart the night, making sleep impossible and torturing me with thoughts that the gods were speaking in disapproval.

I awoke savoring the pure, sweet smells of the wet desert plants and rocks. The rain had waned to a drizzle, but the skies were still smoking billows of malignant violet, dense as wool. I waded through the mud to fetch my old reliable Minolta for a shot of the sunrise, but my camera seized. Even with fresh batteries and film, it wouldn't advance. Though the Hopis had steadfastly insisted photos of Sipapu were not allowed, I refused to see this for anything more than it was—a freak breakdown, and the loss of the only chance for image coverage of my quest. Of no further relevance was the fact that my watch was suddenly also broken. I was stepping into a timeless zone, and some higher power seemed to be signaling that tracking minutes and hours was a frivolous pursuit here. I dumped all my wet and mucky gear in the back of my rented truck and took off to the southwest, a Hopi cardinal direction, abandoning Tom's useless instructions and using only the compass as my guide.

In minutes I came to the end of the road, the blunt edge of a great canyon. With a sweep of my head I could see high buttes, mesas, table mountains, cathedral spires, stone minarets, tortuous towers, and palisades that seemed to tear the sky. With some orienteering, I could see that the Salt Trail Canyon tumbled into the Grand Canyon a couple miles to the northeast. Trundling across the wasteland I found a trailhead, shouldered my pack, and headed down 3,000 feet into this Paleozoic pit, as deep as the Grand Canyon at its famous South Rim overlook, but half again as narrow.

It was the steepest descent I'd seen into the Canyon, nearly vertical down a jumble of angular sandstone blocks. The Hopis used ropes made of braided strands of bighorn sheep hide to negotiate this trail. I couldn't image how they navigated it on the return, carrying huge sacks of salt weighing thirty pounds or more up the steep trail. It rained off and on throughout the descent. The rain was a mixed blessing, as it kept temperatures uncharacteristically cool and made it possible to collect rainwater in potholes in the naked rock, but it also made for slippery and dangerous going. The air was suffused with the aroma of cliffrose, reminiscent of the fragrance of spiced honey.

It was a thrill to be back hiking through terrain that was once my backyard. I said hello to the whiptails and the brightly colored Western collared lizards, felt the familiar touch of the tall spike of the Utah agave, brushed by honey mesquite trees, Mormon tea, and the deadly jimsonweed, and avoided the prickly-pear and the Engelmann hedgehog cacti. After three hours I had dropped through layers of Hermit Shale and Supai Sandstone and had leveled out into a sinuous hallway of Redwall Limestone. The limestone cradled pools of light-green water, ideal for a desert dip, but I pressed on, knowing that I only had a limited amount of daylight to reach my goal.

After four hard hours of scrambling, eyes stinging with brow salt, I finally made it to the confluence with the river known as Paayu. From here it would be just two miles downstream to Sipapu.

But something was terribly wrong. Paayu was legendary for its translucent blue-green waters, the result of the magnesium salts and calcium carbonate picked up as the river scours a passage from northeastern Arizona's White Mountains down through the redwall limestone. Yet, as I spread apart a curtain of bright yellow tamarisk, I saw a river angry-red with the blood of sediment and silt flushed by the squalls of the past few days. The river was flowing fast at the edges, while in the deeper middle it bubbled up like thick red porridge. The normal seethe and suck of the river was a lurid roar.

The wind began to bluster, and gusts of sand swirled before me, stinging my face. Lightning split the sky. Volleys of thunder shook the ozone-packed air. Paayu was in flood. It raced by, overflowing its banks. This was a problem, as the trail down to Sipapu was now underwater. I could, no doubt, scratch a way along the canyon walls, or even wait until the floodwaters subsided.

Instead, I stripped naked, as Hopis were supposed to do when visiting Sipapu, and jumped into the red water to consider the situation. I shivered in the thick, cold water, my back against the pummeling current. Perhaps, I thought, the endless streams of obstacles thrown in my path were intended as a message. Perhaps I really was not meant to see Sipapu. Perhaps it would be for the better.

An hour I soaked in the gritty waters as a Monarch butterfly played around my head. I decided to leave my quest unfulfilled and head back out. After waiting twenty-five years and traveling more than a thousand miles, I was going to turn back, two miles and two hours short of my goal. It was the only thing to do.

Humbled, I got dressed. I stepped over a canyon tree frog, listened to the happy descending trill of a Canyon wren, and started the long, slow slog upward. At first it rained, hard, and I knew that, somewhere, Hopi were dancing. At sunset I arrived at the rim and started to drive east across the open desert. A bright double rainbow spilled in front of my hood, a sight so wondrous I had to stop the car. For a few exquisite moments, I didn't harbor longings for my devised objective. Sipapu, like the pot at the end of a double rainbow, was a now a personal manifestation of the unattainable, existing as a perpetual destination, or not at all, the ideal form of a sacred place.

As I turned the ignition key and jounced toward the kaleidoscopic arches, I decided the vision through my windshield was either a grand visual parting gift, offered in gratitude for leaving well enough alone, or a bright beaming path to the next world.

PATAGONIA

PATAGONIA, CHILE
*Wild and free guanaco, once almost eliminated for European
sheep, graze beneath Los Cuernos del Paine in the great Chilian
park at the foot of the hemisphere.*

PATAGONIA
Under the Horns of a Dilemma

The day breaks and asks me:
"Do you hear the lingering water,
The water, over Patagonia?
And I reply: "Yes, I hear it."
   Pablo Neruda
   "I Awaken Suddenly in the Night Thinking about the Far South"

I know it when I see it.
   Former Supreme Court Justice Potter Stewart

In faraway places, there are always familiar faces. I thought I recognized his movements, the nape of his neck. Hesitantly, I walked across the floor of the Carlos Ibanez Airport, in Punta Arenas, the sandy point at the tip of South America on the Strait of Magellan. He turned, and yes, it was him, it was Frenchy, a veteran adventure guide, one I had recruited into the fold so many years ago. We gave one another a guide-hug, one filled with hearty slaps and exaggerated gestures, and simultaneously asked the same question: "What are you doing here?" He had just completed a trek through western Patagonia; I was just arriving for same. "Did you hear the news?" he asked. "The boat that crosses Lago Grey just sank; thirty people almost drowned."

At first I was alarmed: "Oh my god. What happened? Was anyone hurt?" I queried. But when I heard more details, discovering that nobody was hurt—it was just a scare—I felt a twinge of resentment. Just a few days before, Leo LeBon, the seasoned Patagonian explorer, had unrolled a map in his Berkeley living room. He pulled his finger across Lago Grey and announced that with the new boat, one could reach the famous Grey Glacier in minutes, rather than the several days it took by foot. That was good news, I felt, as I had less time than I wanted to explore this landscape on the cone of the southern continent, and the boat would allow me more terrain.

While I was still digesting the news, the boarding call for Frenchy's flight came, and as he pulled on his pack he said, "I would never cross that lake on a boat. It's too dangerous." I thought the words odd coming from an adventure guide, one who had rowed some of the biggest rapids in the world for his job. Yet, as I pondered his reaction, I reconsidered. One person's thrill is another person's danger. I knew several extreme mountaineers, who regularly risked their lives in the high mountains, who would never consider riding a Class V rapid, believing wild water too random, beyond their ken. And being tossed about in ice-cold lake water at the bottom of the continent is not generally appealing, even to the most seasoned adventurer.

I walked to the parking lot, stepped into the back of a Ford Club Wagon piloted by a guide from the lodge where I would be based, and started up the Carretera Austra. Though the van was barely three months old, the front windowpane was cracked and scratched from the hard driving here. The ride was rough, the steppe scenery bleak and monotonous, and I managed to nod off, awaking almost three hours later as we reached the halfway point, the fishing village of Puerto Natales, on the shores of Seno Ultima Esperanza (Last Hope Sound). Black-necked swans were gaggling in front of the ocean-side cafe where we parked.

Inside, a bespectacled, pony-tailed, piratical figure sat hunched over a table. He was Arian Manchego, twenty-eight years old, half-Peruvian, half-Belgian, the chief guide for the Explora Lodge in Torres del Paine National Park, the half-million-acre park and UNESCO biosphere reserve that was our ultimate destination. I sat across from

Arian, and over an avocado sandwich asked if he had heard anything about the Lago Grey boat. He bellowed the laugh of a big-bellied bartender, spermy and muscular, but then suddenly went graven, and the blood seemed to drain from his face. He had been there, he said. Then he described the events leading to the accident.

It happened Sunday, January 30, three days earlier. It was his first charter on the boat, which had just started service the week before. He was guiding a group of twenty-four seniors—he guessed the average age to be sixty—who had just completed an Antarctica cruise and were enjoying a rest day before heading home. It was to be a two-hour cruise, and while returning from Grey Glacier, the wind had picked up. The lake was chopped with five-foot-high whitecaps, yet the captain continued to gun the boat as though it were gliding on a glassy pond. Worse, someone had neglected to tie the bowline, which somehow uncurled under the boat and caught in the propellers of the two outboards. At 12:30 P.M. the boat did a brick-wall stop, and dove like a missile into the trough of a wave. The glacially cold water washed in and the boat almost went over, in the middle of a 250-foot-deep lake.

For the next few hours the boat drifted. Both outboards were shot, and there were no back-ups. Several times the boat almost capsized, but finally it drifted close to the southeastern shore, and there, Peter Metz, an escort for the Antarctica group, made an heroic leap into the water, fully clothed, rope in hand, and swam to the jagged shore. There he managed to secure the line, and as the boat crashed against a shoreline cliff, he and Arian helped the passengers to shore. At 9:30 P.M., nine hours after the ordeal began, the last passenger staggered into the Explora Lodge.

"I will never go on a boat on Lago Grey again," Arian announced at the end of his tale. I believed him, but again was a bit surprised at the severe reaction. After all, this was the wilderness, and, by definition, the only thing predictable is that the unpredictable will happen, and the only adventure is the well-planned itinerary gone wrong.

It was after dark when we arrived in Torres del Paine National

Park, and as I exited the van I met the frigid, fire-hose-force wind for which Patagonia is so renowned. This was latitude-with-an-attitude weather, 51 degrees south, blowing north from Antarctica. It slapped my face, stung my hands, and I had to bend at a 45-degree angle to push a walk. Some months previous I had figured I had spent about a quarter of my adult slumber life in a sleeping bag, and I had always assumed when I came to Patagonia I would do the same. But now, as I slipped through the double doors of the Explora Lodge, I was happy I wasn't setting up a tent. As I entered the lobby, it was like going from the tornado of Kansas to Oz.

The Explora Lodge was a marvel. Warm, clean, and luxurious, its interior panels were all hand-tooled and finely polished, and in the hall, smooth-sloping curves published a delicate scent of cypress. Though there are just thirty rooms in the lodge, there were forty staff members, and one immediately led me down a Swiss sisal carpet to a sacrament of rich Chilean red wine waiting alongside pickled partridge, pork terrine, and grilled lamb, all set on British porcelain. A buffet proffered scallops mousse, *pastel de choclos* (Chilean chicken corn casserole), corvina fish with tarragon sauce, salmon carpaccio, baked rabbit, stuffed artichokes, Roquefort–spinach ravioli, and papayas stuffed with kiwi. This was a cry from my usual freeze-dried camping fare. And after dinner, I collapsed on a soft bed plumped up with a white pique bedspread covering goose-down pillows and crisp cotton Barcelona sheets. It reminded me—I was long overdue in taking my sleeping bag to the dry cleaners.

But it was morning that made the impression. I awoke to a choice austral summer day, and the finest double-glazed window view I had ever seen, in real life or on the last page of *Condé Nast Traveler:* an unencumbered vista of Lago Pehue, a lake the color of a tropical lagoon; of Los Cuernos del Paine, the angular gray and black Paine Horns, sculpted by 12 million years of ice and wind; and of the Torres del Paine, the impossibly vertical spires after which the park is named. Not only was the panorama from my bed something from a middle-Earth imagination, but the architects of the hotel, Germand del Sol and Jose Cruz, had cleverly cut a window through the bathroom wall, so I could relax in the Jacuzzi bath or sit on the toilet and be visually regaled as needles of granite pierced icy skies.

The view was so compelling I was late to my appointment in the lobby. There, in front of a giant fireplace, I met Alejandra Manalla, my guide for the day, and something about her struck me immediately. She was tall, thin as a camel's neck, a bit gangly, with glasses and big brown eyes. She was eighteen-and-a-half years old (her emphasis on the half), and working as a guide during her summer away from college, where she was studying to be a writer. Pablo Neruda, the great Chilean poet, was a role model for her, and I told her he had influenced me as well, and in fact I had made a pilgrimage to his Santiago house just a few days previous.

As we discussed this, we were trundling down the road to Guarderia Lago Sarmiento, and during one bump I suddenly recognized something: She reminded me of me. I, too, was eighteen-and-a-half when I first became a guide, I was studying to write, and I was tall, spectacled, lanky, and quite unsure of myself. She seemed more confident than I my first season, until I asked her about a series of scratches and wounds on her hand and wrist. She turned pale, then told me she had scratched herself while hiking through a tangle of calafate plants. But red abrasions across her skin belied that explanation, so I asked again. Her eyes bored into mine, and she revised her story. She revealed she tore her skin trying to climb from the Lago Grey boat as it was crashing against the cliff. Then she described her version of the events of the Sunday before.

She had nodded off before the boat first crashed into the trough, but then found herself in the role of guide. She did all she could to keep the clients unafraid, though she was more scared than she had ever been, and thought she was going to die. When she finished her account she looked at me and said with some authority, "I will never go on a boat in Lago Grey again. Never."

As if to punctuate Alejandra's conclusion, something with a furry version of a Loch Ness monster neck skipped across the road on spindly legs. It was a guanaco, the wild cousin of the llama. I was excited by the sight and asked if we could stop to take a photo, but Alejandra insisted I be patient. She told me male guanacos like to surround themselves with harems and, because of this, there would be greater numbers ahead. She was right, of course. A few minutes later we passed a knot of three guanacos; then a group of a dozen; then a herd of twenty or more. Suddenly they were everywhere, like 250-pound gremlins. Occasionally, one would stare directly at me with its long lashes and Bette Davis eyes, and I felt I could fall into the camelids.

At Guarderia Lago Sarmiento, we exited the van and started to hike among the guanacos. We walked north, toward Guarderia Y Refugio Laguna Amarga, following a wire fence separating the park from an *estancia* (a large ranch). Every now and then we'd find a cinnamon-colored *tulango,* a baby guanaco, caught in the wire, formless as a pricked balloon, yet stiff with rigor mortis. The fence seemed an inhumane intrusion, until Alejandra explained that just a few years ago there were less than three hundred guanacos left in the region. The ranchers in the area had shot the guanacos, who overgrazed their sheep ranchland. But with the establishment of Torres del Paine National Park, fences were erected, and the population within has swelled, so that now an estimated three thousand guanacos roam freely in the shadow of the Torres del Paine.

At one point I lagged behind our group, trying to photograph the silhouette of a woolly guanaco against the palatial cluster of ice-clad peaks and granite teeth. Then a Patagonian red fox waved his glossy tail in the tall grass just a few feet from my camera, and I lightly stepped over for a closer look. I was so close I could feel its hot breath before it scampered away. Where else, I wondered, did wild animals grow up with such an underwhelming fear of man?

After the fox trotted, I heard a tremulous cry from up on the hill. It was Alejandra, calling for me to catch up with the group. Her voice sounded tentative, plaintive, without the authority I associated with guides. But it was effective. I stashed my camera and hurried to catch up. When I arrived, I told Alejandra a story about how I had been in a capsize of a raft on a river in Africa in 1973. I had been the oarsman and made a misjudgment. A man drowned. I was so devastated by the accident I swore to give up guiding, and I did, for a long year. But finally, the art of the wilds I so enjoyed while guiding beset the carpings of reason, and I stepped back onto a raft. And I found a resonance in the river that had never rung before. Alejandra just looked at me with her big guanaco eyes.

As the oblique, orange light of evening bathed the celebrated towers, I returned to the Explora Lodge where I met Peter and Shirley Metz, the escorts for the Antarctica group that had taken the ill-fated cruise across Lago Grey. I had heard Peter was the hero in the epic, in that while the Chilean crew panicked, he kept a cool head, kept the others calm, and when the boat drifted close to shore, he leapt into the water with a painter, swam to the bank, climbed a cliff, and secured the line. Finally, he stayed to assist all the passengers in exiting the boat, and then saw them safely to a pick-up point on Lago Pehue.

This wasn't the first time Peter had acted the hero. He was on the tarmac in Puerto Williams in February 1991, when a chartered LAN-Chile British Aerospace 146 plane, carrying a group of Antarctica-bound tourists, overshot the runway and crashed into the Beagle Channel. Peter was in the plane in minutes, pulling out survivors and bodies. Of the seventy-two on board, nineteen died. And when a Society Expeditions Zodiac capsized in the Tuamotus River of French Polynesia, killing two, Peter was there, and helped get the survivors to shore. Though it appeared Peter possessed an Homeric catalogue of heroism, he was dangerously close to developing a grim reputation of attracting disasters.

Over a salad I asked Peter about the Lago Grey incident. He didn't want to talk about it. "But," I protested, "there are lessons here. Precious lives were saved. You did the right things. Others didn't. Don't you think we could all learn by hearing about this?"

"No. I don't believe anything good can come from talking about such an incident. It would only give more people pause before visiting this region. It would be bad for business." I noticed then there was more than a *soupçon* of vinegar in the salad dressing. And even though we talked and drank deep into the evening, Peter sponged up the possibilities of my gaining his perspective. I didn't feel regret that Peter wouldn't be joining me for the rest of my exploration.

The following day I found myself hiking up to the base of the Torres del Paine with Arian, Alejandra, and several hotel guests. These would be my first steps into the Cordillera del Paine, the thirty-mile-long range adjacent to but geographically separate from the Andes. Like Yosemite, the Paine range was shaped by glacial action during the Pleistocene Epoch. In geological terms, it is an upthrusted batholith, a gigantic bubble of once-molten granite that rose from the center of the earth and was later covered by huge glaciers stretching from the continental ice cap. When the glaciers retreated, they left behind deep gashes in the "bubble," and an uproar of wild peaks that rise like postmodern monuments from the grassy lowlands near sea level.

It was an odd but satisfying hike as we followed the south bank of the cascading Rio Ascensio upward, across bogs of primordial muck where Alejandra's tiny feet left impressions the size of bear paws. The name *Patagonia* was not meant to designate a political unity but rather a land of big-footed Indians, the *Patagones*, as Antonia Pigafetta, chronicler of Ferdinand Magellan's 1520 voyage, named them when he found giant prints near their winter camp. I couldn't help but wonder if the mud here may have been cause of those first impressions, and ultimately the name for a fifth of a continent.

Arian bounced between the four women clients, yet Alejandra kept pace with me, interpreting the natural history, pointing out the 100-year-old lenga trees, the gnarled Magellanic beech, the pale tresses of Old Man's Beard, and the mountain guanaco, while nodding her head at Arian and his flirtations.

"Mountain guanaco?" I played the straight man.

"That's Arian. He always has a harem," she smiled. Even though this was just her second hike up this path, it was evident Alejandra knew a lot. She loved what she was doing, and confessed she couldn't believe how lucky she was to have this job. In some archaeological way, I remembered feeling that way.

After crawling over the crest of a steep scree slope, I lifted my eyes to a sky full of mountains: Torre Nord (7,400 feet), Torre Sur (8,200 feet), and Torre Central (8,100 feet), looking like colossal crystals growing side-by-side just across a small alpine lake set in a white-streaked cirque. The microclimates of Patagonia showed their range and speed, with one moment bright and sunshiny, the next dark and blustery, the striated spires perforating boiling black clouds. A silence deep as an iceberg swept in and remained, hovering around us. When I glanced over at Alejandra, her eyes seemed to reflect all the wonder of a new world.

Saturday I signed up for a horseback ride. I had expected Arian, but he took the day off, pleading neurasthenia. This time my guide was Giovanna Raineri, twenty-three, from Santiago. She had worked the year before in the Chile Pavilion at the Universal Exposition in Seville, and there met the owners of Explora, who invited her to come join the staff as a guide. She had the adamantine look of an outdoorswoman, and exuded confidence as we rode along the lapis-tinted Paine River. We passed wind-twisted trees, zigzagging *nandues* (flightless ostrichlike birds, also known as Darwin rheas), *liebres* (European hares), a *cingue* (Patagonian skunk), and a sparkling spring, where the water tasted like swamp juice.

At one point I asked Giovanna if she had been in the notorious boat, and a panicked look sped across her face. "Yes, I was there. It was the most frightening episode of my life. I will never step on a boat on Lago Grey again," she said, and she kicked her heels into the side of her steed and galloped ahead, the wilderness guide turning a back on wildness. No one, it seems, is more trapped inside the armature of signs than the signmaker.

At lunch, over a Magallanes-style lamb and vegetable barbecue cooked over glowing beechwood coals, Alejandra showed up at the *quincho* to help. After a couple of pisco sours, I asked if she would join us for the afternoon ride. She said she didn't really know how to ride, but sure, she would love to. After a quick lesson, Alejandra mounted her horse and trotted alongside. We rode to a small waterfall, and scrambled up some slippery rocks to a ledge above the main pool. Alejandra told me that just a few days before, the Explora's chief driver, Pedro, had jumped into the pool, not knowing how to swim. He flailed around for a bit but made it to shore, and emerged smiling. Alejandra seemed impressed, as though she had witnessed the tintinnabulation of a new spirit, one that collaborated with the forces at the bottom of the world.

The following day we made arrangements to visit the Valle del Frances, an enclosed sanctuary deeply incised into the Cordillera del Paine. But in order to get there we would have to take a boat across Lago Pehue; then we would ride horses for several miles, to the Italian Camp, and finally hike the final pitch to the foot of the French Glacier. I had hoped Alejandra would join us, but she wasn't in the lobby, and I wondered if it was just too soon for her to cross another lake.

This time my guide was Pepe Alarcon, a small, quiet man, and of course, as had become a cicadan rhythm, I expected to hear his personal reactions to the boating accident. But as we loaded the launch, I asked Pepe about the incident, and he turned to me and said he had no reactions; he wasn't there. In fact, he was in the Explora Lodge, helping to coordinate the rescue by radio.

Just as the outboards kicked over, Alejandra came running down the pier and jumped on board. She was barely breathing through her crinkly smile, despite the 100-yard dash, and I told her I admired the streamlined fitness of youth. She looked back at me, exploring my face through her glasses, and said, "But you know, I really like wrinkles." And I imagined I had the look of a whelk washed up on a beach.

The crossing was easy. Someone had turned the Patagonian fan off, and the lake, which has no fish, was flat as a griddle. Soon we were saddled up and loping our way into the mountains. This time Alejandra seemed at home on her horse, and she trotted ahead, leaving me in the rear, but always looking back to check my progress. We parked our horses at the Italian Camp, enjoyed a picnic lunch, then took off by foot to reach the high vantage.

As we arrived at the crest of the walk, a lime-green *cachana* (Austral parakeet) zipped over my shoulder, and the mountain began to tremble. If the flap of a butterfly's wing in Osaka can affect the weather in Kansas, imagine what a parakeet can do in the beefy wind of Patagonia. The bird may or may not have contributed, but several loud noises boomed across the valley. I turned my head and watched a series of avalanches spill from the upper reaches of the French Glacier, which flows from the Paine Grande Massif (10,600 feet), the highest point in the Paine fretwork. The glacier itself was a spectacular mass of ice and snow, splintered with deep canyons and jagged pinnacles, a bristling blue. I turned again and looked up into the smooth-walled Gothic Towers, and with another quarter turn I looked down on the pearl-colored waters of Lake Nordenskjold. It was all savagely beautiful.

On the way back a williwaw hit, and the tableau of sharp relief we'd enjoyed on the ride up was now a canvas of gray vagueness. I slouched in my poncho like Lee Marvin in the movie *Cat Balloo,* bringing up the rear, sometimes getting lost. Then I would see an orange blaze painted on a tree or rock, and I'd be back on track. Alejandra was directly in front of me, and I tried to call out her name, but the wind sucked it up and tossed it with the rain toward the Towers behind me, which, wrapped in clouds, now looked bent, like huge mourners at a funeral. Once we got to the shores of Lago Pehue the wind cranked up its battering, the rain its lashing. Whitecaps whipped across the lake. Several Andean condors, the world's largest flying birds, traced curves across the leaden sky like spirits slipping by.

We boarded the boat and set out for the forty-five-minute crossing. As we plunged through the gray-green swells, the boat pitched and reeled. Alejandra sat across from me, looking stern beyond her youth and deep in thought. Then her face lifted like a balloon, her eyes darkly bright, and she threw me a weatherburned smile: "You know, I think I *would* go back on a boat on Lago Grey." And I knew then that, somewhere in the mountain landscape of this woman, there was a magic glass into which she had stepped as a human, and come out a guide.

THE INCA TRAIL

THE INCA TRAIL
Lost City, Lost Stories

Great things are done when men and mountains meet.
William Blake

Each time I return to Machu Picchu, my grandfather, Hiram Bingham, who died when I was a boy, becomes more alive for me. It was his destiny to uncover this mystery center, which now is drawing people from all over the world. He could not have done this without the people of Peru. He listened to the many stories he heard and took them seriously. Others may have dismissed them as dreams or fantasies, but he followed the stories to this place. Now each modern person who comes here with an open heart has a chance to deepen his own story. The meaning of life is visible in the stones, for those who have eyes to see.

E. Benjamin Bingham

While at a travel conference in Washington, D.C., I found myself sharing a drink with a woman who was an accomplished mountaineer. She told me a story about a friend, Yossi Brain, a former journalist for London's *Evening Telegraph*. He had moved to South America, where he wrote some well-regarded books on trekking and climbing in Ecuador and Bolivia. Then, while attempting to climb a peak called El Presidente, in Bolivia's Cordillera Apolobamba, an avalanche hit, carrying Yossi to his death. On the other end of the rope was the woman sharing a drink with me. She miraculously survived, and dug Yossi up from his icy grave. She told me Yossi had two unfulfilled dreams when disaster struck: He had hoped to marry his climbing companion, and he had hoped to write a book on adventure in Peru. "Lost stories," she sighed. I watched her words bead up and roll off her soul.

For many years I ran an adventure travel company, and one of the recurring themes I witnessed was that of the lost story. It came in many forms: the friends and family who couldn't make a trip for conflicts; those who cancelled on the eve for last-minute crises; even those who made the trip but lost a camera or journal, and with it memories. Every trip is a story, with a distinct beginning, middle, and end, replete with challenges, conflict, romance, and resolution. Somehow I find it vexing when a story is lost. Like a light extinguished, I wonder where it went, and what was missed.

One of my company's popular offerings was a guided trek along the Inca Trail to Machu Picchu in Peru. But, though I had overseen a hundred departures to the fabled Lost City of the Incas, I had never made the trek myself. Machu Picchu seemed like a place I would go when my life was no longer in transition, a place to go when my life made sense, so I could absorb the theology the place promised with an uncluttered, quiet soul. Yet, as time passed, I realized I was always in transition, that I had forever been reconnoitering the lower slopes of a magnum opus, that I was perhaps missing my own short satori.

When I heard about Yossi's accident and his undone project in Peru, something clicked. I resolved not to wait. I needed to fill in the space of my own tales not yet told, and Peru and its trail that leads to a city of lost stories seemed the place to pursue them.

So it was I organized a trip with fourteen friends to make the quest, and see first-hand the extravagantly scenic jungle outpost that is South America's most famous living mystery. A counter-programmer by nature, I scheduled our journey for the end of the rainy season, when relatively few dared attempt the high-altitude trail, and condensed the usual four- to five-day trek to just three—a power trip. As with almost every adventure group departure, there was a last-minute lost story. Bill, an Oscar-nominated screenwriter, emailed on the eve that he had been called to Russia by Harrison Ford to work on script—a lame excuse if ever I heard one.

When I left my "out-of-office" message on my email, in some Freudian slither I mistakenly transposed a couple letters: "Off to the Inca *Trial,* and the *Scared* Valley of the Inca," my memo explained, more accurately than I knew.

After various all-night flights from the United States, we congregated in a transit lounge at the Jorge Chavez International Airport in Lima. It was great to see my friends, a gallimaufry of vivid personalities. Many were in a state of transition as well—in jobs, in relationships, in identity, in working out their own stories—and the concept of a pilgrimage to the sacred geography of Machu Picchu had a common resonance. I knew from experience that wonderful things pass through people who explore: unusual things happen; life-changing things. One emerges different from whence he began, transformed, transcended, and with a pack stuffed with stories. Many times clients called to thank me for discoveries made while adventuring, and I had my own lockerfull of discoveries as well.

The reunion was almost short-lived, though, as I came close to missing the Lan Peru flight to Cuzco. My watch had stopped—I was, after all, about to enter a timeless zone—and in my muddle-headed state I misplaced my ticket, so I had to buy another minutes before departure. The pilot held the plane, though, and soon we were off, flying southeast into the Andes, sipping syrupy Inka Kola, watching the mountains grow. An hour later we descended into a bowl of red hills, dipped over a giant white statue of Christ with arms outstretched, swooped over rows of red-tiled rooftops, and landed in the "Navel of the Earth," Cuzco, the ancient capital of the Incas. Supposedly the oldest continuously occupied settlement in the Western Hemisphere, Cuzco is also one of the world's highest cities, at an elevation of more than 10,000 feet.

On tap in the terminal was complimentary *mate de coca,* tea made from the leaves of the coca tree, a brew to help control *soroche,* the nausea and headaches of altitude sickness. Feeling a bit woozy, we gathered our bags, then trundled into Cuzco. Out the windows, Cusquenians smiled and waved at us, a far cry from the image I had from newspaper accounts of terrorists running around the highlands.

For much of the last twenty years, Peru was the leper of South American tourism because of two violent terrorist organizations that roamed the countryside, Sendero Luminoso and the Tupac Amaru Revolutionary Movement. Today these groups have been essentially defeated by government policies put in place by Alberto Fujimori, when he rose to the presidency in a dark-horse campaign in 1990. But a few months prior to our trip, after massive administrative corruption had been exposed, Fujimori fled to Japan, where he faxed in his resignation. His henchman/spy chief, Vladimiro Montesinos, fled to Venezuela, where he underwent plastic surgery and, some say, vowed revenge in some disguised way.

We drove through Cuzco, past tree-lined squares, splashing fountains crowded with pigeons, and grandiose Spanish cathedrals built atop the Incas' stone walls. Then down we went, on a road that spiraled like the shell of a nautilus, into the Sacred Valley to the town of Urubamba, a town of beer, judging from the number of storefronts with red bags on the ends of long poles posted out front, a sign that a batch of *chicha,* the potent fermented corn beer popular in the region, was brewing inside. The beer supposedly induces strength and is an aphrodisiac, and, judging by the number of kids darting around, it works.

We parked at the Posada del Inca, near the Urubamba River. The recommendation was to rest this first day at altitude, but not this group; some went hiking, others horseback riding, others to explore a nearby ruin, and with two others I went mountain biking, and drank Cerveza Cusquena, a commercial local beer (as opposed to *chicha*). At dinner, over a pink trout from the Urubamba River, we listened to an Andean minstrel, whose repertoire included

"El Condor Pasa," the doleful Peruvian tune to which Simon and Garfunkel added their own lyrics:

"I'd rather be a hammer than a nail,

Yes I would, if I only could, I surely would."

It seemed a theme; I had come to believe, from my years talking to clients, that many people who come to Machu Picchu dream of being something different. Such imaginings had crept into my dreams, and perhaps that was a reason for my pilgrimage as well.

Next morning, after lumbering down a Class IV dirt road, outstanding in the number and quality of its ruts, we went rafting. We were negotiating one of the few navigable pieces of the muddy, swollen Urubamba, the river that defines the Sacred Valley. One story has it the Incas held the Urubamba sacred, believing that reflections in the water were fertile fluids from *Mayu,* the Milky Way. It certainly is a productive place. The valley produces twenty-four types of grain, including the rare quinoa, or "Inca rice," a tiny seed high in protein but with no cholesterol that sells for high prices in health-food stores in the United States. At every turn we looked up to see impossibly steep squares and terraces etched into the hillsides, a quilt of maize, beans, barley, onions, figs, tomatoes, pineapples, and, way up high, some of the two hundred different varieties of potatoes grown here. Between the fields were patchworks of several shades of green—groves of eucalyptus—and exposed walls of granite and basalt. And above the valley was the pictorial gravy of high, snow-capped peaks wreathed in puffs of white cloud, framed by golden shafts of light.

I captained one of the rafts, and spent too much time gawking upward. As an Aplomado falcon soared over me, catching canyon updrafts, I hit a wave off-center and the raft climbed the crest like a monkey, then skidded on a bright pitch of foam. The raft would have capsized but for the quick actions of Patty, mother of a professional river guide, who did an heroic high-side that pushed the raft back down.

After the short run we enjoyed a lavish lunch in a riverside tent, featuring brochettes of peppered chicken, big Peruvian potatoes, fresh vegetable salad, local white and red wine, and *paracay,* roasted white-corn kernels so large they looked like the result of a nuclear accident. Outside the tent a stout Peruvian woman, who looked old enough to be an Incan, approached us, and with her eyes seemed to telegraph some code across the ages. She was dressed in a voluminous red and black skirt with double braids falling beneath her hat, her leathery skin toughened by the winds and ultraviolet rays that come with living at altitude. When we offered her some of our large corn, she gave us a magic smile that lit up the valley.

In the afternoon we set out to explore our first Incan ruin, the fortress city of Pisac, high above the Urubamba, overseeing the valley from both directions as well as a trail to the jungle beyond. Looking around, it was impossible not to wonder how an ancient civilization built a city on such precipitous ground. Some of the rocks were the size of Ford Explorers, and they had been quarried in the valley and carried to this promontory. Without cranes or pulleys, building such structures required the use of huge levers, earthen ramps, massive wooden rollers, and lots of muscle, or so the scholars guess. And the giant interlocking blocks of native granite fit so precisely that, even now, a credit card wouldn't fit between them. How did they do it?

Pisac was one of a string of cities, placed strategically a day or two's march apart, that formed the backbone of the far-flung empire. In the early 1400s, the Incas succeeded in uniting the individual tribes that spanned the Andes, from Peru to Bolivia to Ecuador and Chile, westward into the coastal deserts and eastward into the Amazon basin, creating the greatest civilization known in South America before European arrival. But in 1532, a crisis over the leadership of the empire coincided with the arrival of Spanish conquistadors, opening the way for it to fall. The Spanish looted and destroyed the empire's cities, and, although the Spaniards were greatly outnumbered, they massacred all who resisted.

In their haste to plunder Inca gold, the Spanish failed to find a small stone city, 8,000 feet in the clouds, hidden in a ring of peaks, downriver from Pisac. Legend has it that the gods of the Sacred Valley of the Inca protected it. The lost city, Machu Picchu, was our goal.

Below the ruins of Pisac, the eponymous village was thick in its Sunday Mercado, and we arrived in time for the last hour of trading. Women wrapped in brightly colored woolens, with long black plaits hanging from beneath bowler hats, presided over blankets piled high with stacks of onions, tomatoes, bananas, potatoes, and corn. In another quarter were the tourist trinkets: soft alpaca sweaters and rugs, colorful caps and hats, drawstring bags, purses, masks, wall hangings, chess sets with opposing pieces representing conquistadors and Incas, finger puppets, and walking sticks with grinning, bucktoothed Inca men carved into the handles. I was intrigued by the artwork from the self-proclaimed "Picasso of Pisac," but ended up buying only some coca leaves and a lime wedge that, in combination, locals claim provides stamina and helps stem altitude sickness.

That night Peter Bohm, our lead guide, gathered the group and formally introduced us to our other two guides, Manolo Lazo, celebrating his twentieth year on the Inca Trail, and twenty-three-year-old Juan Carlos Yanez Choquehuanca, son of a well-known local guide. Manolo, tall and with a profile that cut like a condor, was a romantic and mysterious figure, so handsome and vague that clients could pin any fantasy they liked onto him.

Peter then handed out small duffels, telling us that, because of new rules, we would each be restricted to twenty-two pounds for the trek, including sleeping bag and all clothing and gear. This seemed impossible to me, but even more so to others, some of whom had gone on shopping sprees before the trip and had luggage bulging with new gear. We were dispatched to repack, then we retired to the bar for pisco sours, the liquid franca of Peru, and renditions of "I'd rather be a hammer than a nail."

The following day began with a wide-eyed ride on a narrow-gauge railroad through an ever-narrowing gorge. The Inca armies fled this way in the sixteenth century, and the vast stores of gold they carried and hid in the jungles have never been found. Generations of adventurers and explorers have followed this valley in search of hidden treasure. So were we, in some fashion.

Out the window the river grew angrier and wilder, a liquid chaos of overfalls and mushroom boils that made me shiver. Over the years I had run my fair share of extreme white water, but never had I seen stretches as powerful and mad as this. Years ago, back in the United States, while reviewing maps of the Urubamba I had fantasized about boating the river down to Machu Picchu. Now I saw this would be a thankfully lost story.

We decanted west of the town of Ollantaytambo, at kilometer eighty-eight on the line and trailhead to the high and mighty trek. Here thirty *seminarians,* Indian descendants of the Incas, lean, brown, and hard-muscled as pumas, shouldered our tents, cooking gear, food, medical kits, and personal effects and started scuttling up the path, hunched under burdens as big as they. Much of the hiking advice doled to us by guidebooks and previous trekkers these porters defied: most were hatless, and wore thin clothing and black sandals made from used tires—and not a water bottle in sight.

In minutes the porters were meandering dots on the trail above us, colored pins marking the way to the horizon. We shouldered our puny day packs, crossed a wobbly suspension bridge, and began stepping back in time, up the five-hundred-year-old trail. We toddled over undulating *puna* grasslands and through a small *polylepis* forest above the Urubamba roiling in the gorge below. In the distance, the snow-capped, 20,000-foot peak of Mount Veronica shimmered as though it were a mirage.

I stopped for a second to adjust my pack and heard nothing but sweet birdsong, swallows and parakeets. At last, far away from the tourist restaurants and bars where it was an ongoing refrain, there would be no more versions of "I'd rather be a hammer than a nail" for the next three days. But because we were at the tail of the rainy season, the trail was blooming with visual base notes: orchids, wild iris, yellow hoya, impatiens, geraniums, and galadia, which were hovered over by giant hummingbirds.

Village children along the trail, some with the long red petals of the *kantu* (the Peruvian national flower) hanging from their hats, scampered out to greet us and ask for *carmella* (candy), but we did them one better: Lisa, founder of an ethno-pharmaceutical company, hands out toothbrushes, which left them thankful but puzzled.

At the ruins of Patallacta, where the stones were stacked like loaves of bread, we broke for a tented lunch of fresh vegetables and chicken salad with hot tea, coffee, and coca, then continued on. The hiking patterns were starting to set: avid-outdoorsfolk Brian and Janine out front, the middle-ground with ever-shifting couples, and the rear with Patty and Carrie, two women of polymathic achievements, and the more contemplative of the group.

The trail, more defined now, was a remnant of one of the most extensive road networks that laced the ancient world. It steepened as we continued up the Cusichaca Valley, passing scattered mud-brick homes with clusters of the usual icons on top—a Catholic cross, two bowls, two pots for cooking, two bottles for drinking, and stairs, offerings to the gods. When we passed one with a Coke bottle on top, Patty didn't miss a beat: "The gods must be crazy."

At the Andean community of Huayllabamba, at 9,800 feet, we stopped for a proper rest. Here, when I bolted back a cloudy glass of the infamous homemade *chicha* (which tasted like yogurty cider), I started to hallucinate and saw a bright green parrot on my shoulder. But wait—it wasn't the *chicha*. The rest of the group began yelling, confirmation that a very real bird was pecking away at my hat. I couldn't get him off my shoulder until, finally, the local beer maiden coaxed him down.

Because we were still in the unpopular rainy season, we pretty much had the trail to ourselves. However, at Huayllabamba we met Jane, a solo trekker from New Zealand who had hired a private guide and, coincidentally, was on the same schedule as our group. As she sat for lunch, she pulled out of her guide's pack a prepared peanut butter sandwich, commenting that she had expected something more exotic. Emboldened by the brew, I offered her some. Wisely, she passed.

After the respite we started up a sharp slope, the view ever growing behind us. At about 12,000 feet I began to feel a dull throbbing in my temples, a bit of an altitude headache. I pulled out some of the dried coca leaves, stuffed them in my mouth, and began a chew. But, just to be sure, I also popped a Diamox, a diuretic popular with climbers.

Our campsite, Llulluchapampa, is at 12,700 feet, at the edge of a marshy meadow. I arrived at about 4:00 P.M., in a light drizzle. Other members of the group staggered in over the next couple of hours, with Carrie and Patty arriving just as the sun was slipping away, bathing the jagged pinnacles above us in a golden-haired light. Patty had a touch of altitude sickness, and remarked on how tough the terrain was. Manolo, in his Zen koan way, advised: "Don't hate the mountain; it is you who decided to take this trip."

With all in camp we each set about exploring this new world. Ed, a retired Microsoft executive, tall, buffed, and with a thick mane of hair past his shoulders, camped next to the cliff overlooking Mount Huayanay and the valley where the trail rolled away in waves. When he took off his shirt revealing a Praxitelean body, a couple of the women in our group dashed over to pose. He looked like an Incan god against the Andean backdrop, or a Fabio who had taken a wrong turn at Harlequin Pass. I handed out Andean Mints I had smuggled from the United States, and Joshua, another retired Microsoftee, rolled out his state-of-the-art sleeping bag, but couldn't quite figure out how to get in.

At dusk, as the last rays touched them, the surrounding peaks were suffused with pinks, oranges, then molten gold. The campsite at that moment seemed touched by the divine. Regardless of any spiritual energy, though, the scene was breathtaking, mind-blowing, a magical mixture of vegetation and stone, waterfalls and rainbows, folding mountains and swirling clouds.

Dinner was vegetable soup, sautéed beef and rice, and chocolate pudding—nothing too exotic, until Jane, the solo Kiwi hiker, pulled back the flap of the dining tent and presented me with a dish. Her guide, wanting to accommodate her wish for more interesting fare, had purchased a plump guinea pig on the trail, a delicacy in these parts. Now the roasted pig was on my plate, feet folded in the air, its tiny teeth exposed in a death grin. It had a rare and tangy taste.

Despite the fact that alcohol is not recommended at altitude, Peter presented the group with a bottle of pisco, and we drank deep into the blue night. Here old stories flowed; new ones were uncorked. Dan, a former executive at Teledesic and the hominine analogue to "Ask Jeeves," dazzled us with a near-infinite mental database of knowledge. Janine spun yards of yarns. Brian had bottomless asides. We laughed as hard as hyenas until the bottle was dry.

I staggered to my tent beside a moonlit mountain silhouette. The Big Dipper poked its handle from the northern horizon. To the south, the Southern Cross flew like a kite through the *Mayu*. In this juncture of hemispheres, I felt the convergence of opposing worlds—North and South, old and new, serenity and excitement, bohemian and bourgeois. As the porters tucked in beneath their ragged ponchos, I unzipped my nylon tent, put on my sleeping ensemble of thermal underwear, fleece, and socks, and passed out.

In the middle of the night, John, one of our most strapping members, burst out of his tent and started puking, waking up the rest of camp. Montesinos' Revenge.

Before the dawn was whole I awoke to the sound of singing toads, then heard a light rap on the nylon flap of my tent. One of the porters brought a cup of coca tea and a hot washbasin. Then Manolo urged us to get going with one of his saws: "If you miss the morning, you may waste the day; if you miss your youth, you may waste your life."

We breakfasted on scrambled eggs and porridge as the shadows peeled back from the valley below and the rising light painted the peaks. We then set off on our climb into a protean world, through three vegetation and climatic zones to Dead Woman's Pass, which, at 13,776 feet, is the highest point on the Inca Trail.

It was a grunt, especially the final pitch up a stone staircase into slim air. What has been said of Wagner's music—it has beautiful moments but awful quarter hours—seemed true of this section of the trek. I was panting heavily with every step, and found myself tacking back and forth across the steps like a Spanish galleon under weigh. Some of the steps were so wide apart, and so high, it seemed impossible that the small-statured Incans had designed these for their own barefooted messengers, or armies, or llama trains. What were they thinking?

At last, a step, and we were on top of the world, Ma—highest point on the Inca Trail. On the rocky, tundralike landscape we stood among butter-yellow gorse bushes and wind-battered trees and looked down the path we'd just climbed, then over to the one that unfolded ahead, and to the encircling snow-covered peaks. It occurred to me that this was not just a path, but a work of art. There was nothing coincidental about the dazzling combinations of human-made and scenic beauty, designed as theater, as a series of epiphanies, with the route, passes, and sudden, magnificent views planned for dramatic effect. It was devised, it seemed, to entertain and elevate the soul of the traveler.

As we began the descent, for the first time I appreciated the neat granite edging stones placed as steps. We snaked down toward Pacamayo (Hidden River), where the warm, humid air of the Urubamba rose to create a tropical cloud forest. The plants here forgot their manners and behaved like trees, and the stepping-stones were coated in lichens, roots, creepers, and thick, juicy red and yellow mosses.

A steady clamber took us over the second pass, Runkuraqay, at 12,900 feet, just above the circular ruins of the same name, with an uplifting view back toward Dead Woman's Pass. We then stepped down to the staggeringly situated ruins at Sayacmarca, a stronghold built on an unassailable outcrop between two hanging valleys. After a picnic lunch, we hiked across a third pass—the last—and then down a flagstone path that pitched into a tunnel, carved through solid rock. After a long traverse along a smoothly worn contour line, we rounded a bend and there across the bluff was a line of giant lemon drops: our tents. Minutes later I wandered into our camp at Phuyupatamarca (Town at the Edge of the Clouds), at 11,906 feet, to the smell of freshly popped popcorn, my favorite. I'd reached the Rapture.

But by the time the second wave of our group arrived, clouds had begun to drift over us and the weather had turned cold and wet.

I took coca tea and popcorn in the dinner tent and watched shadows lengthen against a wall. It was getting late, and there was no sign of Jay, at fifty-three the oldest member of our group, or Dan, Patty, Carrie, Juan Carlos, or Manolo. I drank some more, wrote in my journal, finished the bowl. A plump black mosquito flew in lazy circles around my head, as though the meager supply of oxygen hindered its attack mode. By now we had been in camp for two hours with no sign of the rear guard, and the light was evaporating. I shared my concern with Peter, who found some porter volunteers. I gave one my flashlight, and off they went back down the cobblestones.

Twenty minutes passed. I was worried now. Had I designed a trip that was too aggressive?

When forty minutes later there was still no sign I decided to go look, and traipsed back down the trail. But, as the light was fading fast and I had no flashlight, I turned back. After all, I rationalized, everyone on the trip was tough; all had been survivors in the business world. But the combination of altitude and a truly strenuous challenge could take a toll on anyone.

Just as the sun was making its final flash, the porters showed up carrying a body in a sleeping bag. My God, I thought, was it Carrie or Patty? Had our story gone terribly wrong?

It turned out the body was a porter from another group who had passed out drunk on the trail and cut his knee. Dan, a former volunteer firefighter who admitted he knew just enough to be dangerous when it came to medical matters, remembered the ABCs of

CPR: Airway, Breathing, Circulation. Dan checked the downed porter's pulse, his pupils, and his breathing, and, using Jay's medical kit, dressed the wound. Though the porter could have died of exposure on the high trail, now that he'd been rescued his only harm, Manolo assured us, would be a hangover.

Minutes later the final two arrived, Carrie's excitable blond hair flocculent with sweat, Patty's indefatigable grin nobly propped. They were utterly exhausted, but in high spirits. When I asked Manolo if we should forgo the pisco out of respect for the accident and the exhaustion, in his Godfatherlike whisper he said, "If you cry because you can't see the sun, your tears won't let you see the stars." So, we uncorked the pisco.

The porters prepared a special dinner for our final night on the Inca Trail: spaghetti with meat sauce, creamed asparagus, and, for dessert, *masamora morada,* pudding made from local black cornflower.

Then it started to rain. Fat drops spattered the tents all night. It was still raining with the leaden light of morning, and a dense white fog oozed over the valley.

Despite the rain, the hum and buzz of anticipation coursed through our ranks. From here the porters would run ahead and drop off our gear at Machu Picchu. Since we would not see them after pancakes, we participated in the ritual of paying the porters. They lined up, dressed to the eights in traditional shawls and serapes, all in vibrant reds and maroons, and one by one Peter called their names and handed them tip money. When Luis, the twelve-year-old son of one of the porters, came out to receive his first tip ever, the crowd, both porters and clients, erupted in applause.

Soddenly, we unwound the mountain in silence, save for the rustle of raingear and the tap of walking sticks. In a couple hours of hiking we left the wilderness behind as we stepped into the concrete-sided Trekker Hostel, which hosts a bar, a restaurant, hot showers, even television. After bathroom breaks we hiked around the bend to the ruins of Winay Wayna (Forever Young,) which were honed into the hillside like an amphitheater. Along one edge were ceremonial baths, a cascading series of pools. The Incas channeled water from a luminous waterfall that even now runs ceaselessly. Emerging waist-high from a rock wall, each of the fountain's clear streams falls into a pool before being swallowed up again by the rock. This was sculpture, not architecture, and it was all the more remarkable knowing the Incas created this without the use of iron or the wheel, so legend goes.

Here we all stooped into a hoary bath and purified ourselves before making the final steps into the crown jewel of South American archaeology: Machu Picchu. An hour later we traversed a cut in the side of a lush mountain, past delicate ferns, yellow orchids, and rock roses. Then we trudged up a long, steep Incan staircase to a platform with columns straddling a low saddle: Intipunko, the Gateway of the Sun.

Scholars believe Incan religious leaders positioned Intipunko here so that at the spring equinox, every September 23, the light would stream through the gate at dawn. With an exhale I spilled through the gate, and the view was revealed as though a curtain had been pulled away. Below us the white granite and quartz of the most sacred of Inca sites sparkled, its Toblerone-shaped walls and deserted craters stretching over seventy acres. Clinging to a high spur, it sprawled between two somber mountains, or *Apus,* that stood up like green velvet knife blades. Wrapped around this diorama in an inescapable embrace were snow-covered summits, glistening like ice-cream cones, seemingly lighting the storybook city below. The beautiful collaboration between human and nature grabbed me by the scruff of the neck and gave me goose bumps.

About twenty others surrounded us, all subdued in awe, tired eyes wide. Clouds rolled in, then drifted away, creating a constantly changing pattern of light and shadow. It rained for a while; it stopped.

Aching legs, dirty hair, blisters, and bad tempers were forgotten in a second. But we didn't linger long; the gravity of Machu Picchu pulled us downward.

From the gate we walked another two miles, down a path of wide flagstones, passing two llamas nonchalantly nibbling trailside greenery, sentries to the final approach. One of the animals answered Joshua's attempt at interspecies communication with a spit to the face.

A few minutes later we were at the classic vantage, the brochure shot overlooking the mist-shrouded Ciudadela (Citadel) beneath the sharp, jungle-green peaks of the Vilcanota Range, half a mile above the torrent of the Urubamba River. The past suddenly seemed real but just out of reach, like a shiny coin beneath a grate.

I arrived at the edge of the city in tandem with the sun, stretched my arms skyward, and drank in the view. Gray rocks formed the skeleton of a village with a spiritual cast, its masonry beautifully offset by verdant plazas. One can never escape home, though, and as I gazed at the tiers of roofless rooms I couldn't help but think they looked like ancient rows of office cubicles.

The ruins seemed to tell a story, but no one knows exactly what it was. For centuries this mystical Inca bastion sat undisturbed above the clouds, its serenity rippled by little more than occasional llama herdsmen and hovering condors. Then, on July 24, 1911, American explorer and historian Hiram Bingham followed an eight-year-old Indian boy up a mountainside and stumbled upon the haunting, mortarless stonework situated, Bingham said, " . . . in the most inaccessible part of the Andes, so safely hidden in tropical jungles on top of gigantic precipices that the [conquering] Spaniards would not be able to find it unless they were guided to the spot."

Other than a few farmers in the area, no one had been aware that the jungle city existed. Off and on for the next four years, Bingham and a team of archeologists, sponsored by Yale University and the National Geographic Society, cleared away the tangle.

But Machu Picchu, or "Old Peak," in the Quechua language, remained a huge archeological question mark, its origins an enigma wrapped in a riddle. Who built it? Why did they build it? What was its significance? The place, with its 100 stairways and 3,000 steps, seemed a Möbius strip of paradox and indeterminacy.

Juan Carlos gave us his theory, but, he cautioned, it was theory only. The citadel was built in the mid-1400s. Incas may have abandoned Machu Picchu early in the sixteenth century, decades before the Spanish conquest that began in 1532. Spanish chroniclers, piecing together Incan history from the stories of Indian elders, never learned about Machu Picchu. Maybe their informants didn't know it was there. Maybe they chose not to tell.

Many believe this was the religious capital of the Inca empire. Some theorize that specially selected women, "virgins of the sun," were stationed here to serve the Inca rulers. Others think perhaps this was a university, where the Inca religion was studied and priests were trained. Others variously posit it as some sort of refuge, an observatory, a military base, or the legendary El Dorado, the city of gold. Still others think it was a station for an advanced alien race from outer space. Real people had real stories here, intricate tales full of romance, adventure, drama, humor, and tragedy. But now the stories are lost. What actually happened here only the ghosts of the Incas know for sure.

An estimated 600 to 700 people lived in Machu Picchu. Why did they leave, and where did they go? One theory has it there was not enough farmland to sustain a growing population. The site may have run out of water, as an unfinished irrigation project suggests. Some believe a fire swept the mountain. Perhaps the city was the victim of the Inca civil war that ended shortly before the Spanish arrived. Others think Machu Picchu's population fell to European diseases that spread south from Panama. Others think a cataclysmic earthquake struck; two parallel fault lines border the site. Clues slip past like fish in flight.

Since we had arrived by trail, late in the day, we were practically alone as we lorded over the city. As I stood overlooking the imposing sprawl of stone temples, terraces, shrines, and sundials, I kept waiting to "feel the power," the surge of mystic energy suggested in the novel *The Celestine Prophecy.* I fixed my eyes on the sacred city and awaited a metaphysical presence, a cosmic connection, divine inspiration, some ancient magic, harmonic convergence, or some higher infusion of tranquility or transcendence. But nothing came.

Just outside the ruined city, we boarded an aging Mercedes diesel bus that began the grind down the "Zig-Zag Bingham Road," a four-mile, 2,000-foot descent to the riverside town of Aguas Calientes. As the bus grumbled, a small boy in Indian garb plunged into the underbrush and sprinted directly down the mountainside, intercepting the bus after each of the fourteen hairpin turns, with bellowing, half-crazed tribal cries and a peculiar horizontal waving gesture. He continued to appear from the roadside foliage all the way to the bottom. When the bus stopped, he climbed aboard. With a final triumphant whoop he set about collecting money for his show.

Past a gauntlet of souvenir peddlers, we walked up the street as an aroma of corn and baked bread wafted by, mixing with the exhaust of rickety, overloaded trucks and the rush of air from the roaring Urubamba. We turned through a garden dripping with white Georgia O'Keeffe-esque flowers and went into the Machu Picchu Pueblo Hotel. We celebrated that night with pisco sours and the welcoming refrain, "I'd rather be a hammer than a nail."

The next day we bussed back up the ribbon of switchbacks to the sacred citadel for a more formal magical mystery tour, and wondered why the running boy wasn't doing his trick in reverse. As the bus climbed we watched in silence as the sun grazed the surrounding mountaintops and the mists rose from the gorge below, then thinned, layered, and slowly dissolved in the warming air.

As we headed for the fake Inca-style entrance gate, we experienced for the first time "McPicchu": the Lost City as fast-food tour. We jockeyed with hoards of floral-shirted tourists who had taken the seventy-five-mile train trip from Cuzco for a half-day sightsee. More than 300,000 trippers a year troop the ruins this way, from crystal-clutchers to AARP cattle calls, as many as 3,000 a day. Somehow the spell seemed to break with the crowds, and in some elitist way we felt invaded, as though we had earned the right to explore

Machu Picchu, while the teeming train masses had not.

Juan Carlos led us through the maze, adroitly mounting steps and ducking into nooks and crannies, through the fragments of temples and houses. He pointed out the trapezoidal doors and windows, shapes that apparently withstand earthquakes better than squares (so, why aren't there more like these in San Francisco?), and holes that might have supported poles for torches or hangers for decorative objects. We looked at niches where mummies may have been placed in the traditional knees-to-chest position for sacred ceremonies. We peered through exquisitely crafted openings in the Temple of the Three Windows, framing the large main plaza, a broad lawn where archeologists believe markets were held and men played a game similar to field hockey.

Every portion of the site had a name: the Urban Sector, the Fountain District, the Royal Sector, Sector of the Quarries, the Upper Group, the Lower Cemetery, the Industrial Sector, the Jails, and the Temple of the Sun, the only rounded building in Machu Picchu. Here, archeo-astronomers found that a ceremonial window and altar are aligned with the sunrise on the June solstice, with accuracy within two arc-minutes.

There were many more structures and holes, all pieces of a puzzle that has never quite come together. An obelisk near the royal compounds has been identified either as a sundial or an indicator to divine optimal growing seasons. A slab on the floor of an area known as the Condor Group resembles a map of South America. How the Incas could have figured that out nobody knows. This was story as epistemological mystery.

We poked around the Palace of the Princess, the only two-story structure in the labyrinthine site. Juan Carlos pointed out a stone slab with indents for pillows that served as the base of a bed, the trapezoidal door with deep niches for protective log barriers, the shelves that might have held the things that a princess treasured.

As we walked around the citadel past a dozen other guides giving similar explanations to tourists, it seemed that nothing Juan

Carlos was saying was unique or personally interpretative, but in fact part of a common script. Nobody knew the story here, but everyone knew what to say. There was enough sublimation in the neighborhood to power a tram. I hated being herded around a theme park, and fed the corn of practiced lore, so when we reached the north end, I took off for the dark green sugarloaf mountain that looms above the Lost City.

Huayna Picchu, "Young Peak," rises 1,000 feet, lush and symmetrical, girdled by terraces, crowned with a ruin called The Temple of the Moon. The novelist Christopher Isherwood called it " . . . an appalling berg of rock, like the fragment of a fallen moon." Perhaps at such a height I could capture an overview of this vast story, and make some sense of it all, decoding the stories lost to time, and reconciling it with the stories lost by the unexplored. Like a dream not remembered, stories are lost in many ways, but, I realized, it was better to dream and lose a story than to never dream at all.

At a small guarded gate I read the warnings about dizzyingly steep steps, signed the register, and walked down to a small saddle between the ruins and the peak, then started climbing. Straight up. In places the steps seemed suspended in space. I leaned into the rock to give myself a psychological balance against the spiraling emptiness off my shoulder.

Zigzagging up the side of the mountain, I finally reached a short, slanting tunnel. Squeezing through, I reached the top—a pile of boulders, some carved flat. A few feet below, jumping into emptiness, were Inca terraces overgrown with weeds.

But now, looking down, I had a condor's view of Machu Picchu, a sprawling pointillist mural of the world. The arrangement of structures, plazas, and terraced fields looked as if it had been intended as some kind of message. Perhaps it was a place where the forces of the universe converged, what some call a vortex point. In the high postillusional air, I doubted it. Every explanation, no matter how sophomoric or scientific, was speculation. The Incas left no written records.

From my perch I pondered the unanswerables while gazing down at the antlike tourists scurrying among the ruins. However they got there, in hiking boots or high heels, they were creating their own tales, finding their own stories. Below them the Urubamba raced through a horseshoe bend, past a hydroelectric plant, then looked as though it was being fed into a fog. Beyond were rows of green mountains tumbling over themselves, brushed by clouds. In the far distance, in blinding white, towered Nevado Salcantay, an *evado* (glaciated peak), sacred to the Incas. Beyond still were ruins yet to be found, paths yet to be pioneered, landscapes yet to be mapped, and mysteries yet to taunt.

Though the clouds had parted, the view I surveyed atop Huayna Picchu offered no illumination or clarity. It was more like flinging an unbound book onto the floor and asking visitors to sort it out. The missing chapters included information-theory, linguistics, semiotics, structuralism, phenomenology, developmental theory, hermeneutics, iconography, mysticism, and ideology. The only thing I could see clearly was that Machu Picchu cannot be decoded, that it stands in as a metonymic shorthand for the whole universe of lost stories. But, just to be there, in an ancient, ambiguous narrative, I had added a rich chapter to my own story, with friends as protagonists, a quest as tension, riddles of origins as plot points, and a beaming group photo as the satisfying dénouement.

THE LOST ART

BURGUNDY, FRANCE
*Friend and trip leader Eric Blachford notes the road has dead-
ended by the pinot noir*

THE LOST ART

Biking Burgundy

G et a bicycle. You will not regret it, if you live.

Mark Twain

This was not the tour I signed up for. We were lost. We were doubly lost. This was supposed to be a "civilized cycle trip" through Burgundy, on paved secondary roads winding down the *route de grands crus*. Yet Erik, our un-guide, had us stomping through steep, muddy vineyards, holding our customized road bikes above our shoulders, as we sought out asphalt. And we were two hours late for lunch. . . . The plan had promised a moveable feast, but we could find no open bistros, no cafes, no *boulangeries* or *patisseries*, no *traiteurs*, no *brasseries* or *buvettes*, no restaurants, no grocery stores—no open shutters at all on the tall French windows en route. So we were moving, but there was no feast. The creamy-white Charolais cattle we passed were beginning to look pretty good.

After thirty minutes of climbing over fences and crumbling, lichen-covered stone walls and tramping through orderly rows of vines, we again hit pavement and circled down toward the empty stone village of Fixin. Along the way we passed some folks on one of those commercial bike trips so upscale I expected they would be wearing loafers and, when I glanced at their Vuitton panniers, I saw clearly wrought, typed instructions describing in detail every turn and switch to the meter. These folks would never get lost, I was certain, and would be on time for repasts.

Our tour, though, was a private one, cobbled together by Erik, a former guide for the famous biking-tour company Butterfield and Robinson, now a high-tech exec. Though he gathered the group of friends to retrace one of his favorite routes, he expressively submitted that he was not "the guide," not the hand-holder who would pamper us through the countryside. Instead, he would facilitate the journey, marking out rough routes each day, and then we could choose to follow him or go our own ways. His only instructions as we set out this morning were to avoid roads with painted lines and roads marked with an *N,* which were the thoroughfares. Still, I expected a veteran like Erik to keep us on track. Yet, as I tried to decipher his scribbling, I saw that he even misspelled key village names: his *Teruant* was really supposed to be *Terant,* though even that was hard to figure out on the 1/200,000-scale regional maps he issued.

But I was even more lost that evening when we ventured into the cellar vault of the eighteenth-century Chateau Andre Ziltener, in the postcard village of Chambolle-Musigny, for a degustation. Beyond the boulevards of barrels, in a cool, gravel-floored room dim as a church, we tasted the prized Pinot Noirs of the Cote de Nuits. But as others took restrained, birdlike sips, *ooh*ing at the minerally taste distinctions, then dove to the deep waters of organoleptic traits, detecting the *gout de terroir* (taste that is unique to the wine from a specific vineyard), I found I couldn't tell the difference between the 1995 Chambolle-Musigny and the nearly twice as expensive 1996 Bonnes Mares Grand Cru. I had pinot envy.

The greatest workout on the trip was exercising our palettes, and we were champions. That night was our fourth in-country and our fourth four-hour dinner. We found our way to the Aux Vendanges de Bourgogne in the village of Gevrey-Chambertin, and we indulged in a meal so nutritionally incorrect that cardiologists watching would have had heart attacks. We drowned in rich heavy creams, beef, bacon, lamb, game with fur, game with feathers, and duck: breasts of duck, thighs of duckling, duck terrines, foie gras, potatoes cooked in duck, *confits de canard.* And then there were the cheeses: plump rounds of goat cheese, runny Brie, a blue d'Auvergne, the orange rind Epoisses, Gruyère, Camembert, St. Florentin, Soumaintrain, Chaource, Amours de Nuit, Ami de Chambertin, Citeaux, *fromage blanc*—it was impossible to make a decision, and it made it easier to understand Charles DeGaulle's famous remark that "it's impossible to rule a country that makes 250 kinds of cheese."

Even though traditionally the French drink more wine than anyone else—more than sixty liters (sixteen gallons) a person per year, compared to just under seven liters a person in the United States —that night, judging from the dead bottles at the end of the table, we brought the U.S. average up to par.

The next morning, my head doing the postprandial Burgundian thrum, I found myself lost in the inscrutability of French plumbing, trying to shower holding a snake-tube showerhead in one hand and soap in the other. The French excel at technology, what with the Concorde, nuclear power, and the TGV (Tres Grande Vitesse) trains, but bathrooms are stuck in another century, designed for maximum inconvenience. If ever there were an excuse for the revival of the guillotine, this was it.

As we saddled up for the day's ride, I decided to split from the tribe, thinking I could make my way with a better chance of not getting lost by not following others. So I examined Erik's brief instructions and took off with a whirr of derailleur gears.

Of course I got lost and found myself going the wrong way on a one-way street in Nuits St. Georges, with Renaults zipping past as though piloted by Grand Prix driver Alain Prost. One raging driver called me "physical graffiti." So I turned around and followed a French poodle to a bar, where I rolled out my map on a wobbly table covered in checked oilcloth. I ordered a Coke and looked around.

This was the real Burgundy, the rural France of playwright Marcel Pagnol. Though it was 11:00 in the morning, a line of locals was perched on stools like a row of amiable buzzards, big bellies to the bar, tipping back clunky glasses filled with Ricard—the potent, anis-flavored liqueur—and ice water, the drink of Toulouse-Lautrec. I couldn't figure out the best route to our destination, the medieval walled city of Beaune, so I mustered courage and asked a customer, a man in an old shirt and sleeveless vest, with flattened hair, a face the color of red wine, and the nose of actor Jean Reno. He banged his glass on the bar but smiled broadly, baring nicotine-stained teeth, and then traced a route on my map and pointed at a street out the window. Sure enough, in a couple hours I was on the outskirts of Beaune, but had no clue how to find our lodging for the night, the Hotel Le Cep. I wandered about town like a lost puppy until I spied through the crowds a familiar blue and gold biking shirt. It was Lloyd, from our group, biking by. He had spent the previous night at the Hotel Le Cep, so he knew the way, and I jumped on my bike and weaved through traffic, following him home.

That evening I strolled across the way to the Hotel-Dieu (God's House), Beaune's chief tourist attraction. Founded by Nicolas Rolin, a kind of fifteenth-century Patch Adams who hoped to cheer up the poor and the sick with extravagant architecture, it features a dazzling roof of yellow, red, green, and black-glazed Flemish tiles. The splendid hall for the ill, the Salle des Povres, with its pastel ornamented and beamed ceiling built to resemble the upside-down hull of a Viking ship, and the stage-set lineup of elegant beds draped in rich fabric, was terribly inviting, a home for lost and broken souls, and I was tempted to tuck in for a nap. However, the Flemish polyptych of anguished souls depicted in the painting of the Last Judgment showcased the downside of being lost—lost souls were being hurled down to hell. With a settling uneasiness, I changed my mind.

Afterwards it was time for another marathon meal, but I was leery of more multi-course Olympic eating. I felt I was thickening to wine-barrel proportions, so I begged off and wandered down cobblestone streets until I found a simple crêperie. There I ordered a crêpe filled with hamburger and ketchup, *pommes frites,* and a beer, and I kept consumption to less than an hour. It was familiar territory, a meal innocent of heroics, but later that night, as I met my balloon-bellied friends at the bar, they enthusiastically described their epicurean adventures, and all I could say was that the beer was good, the crêpe better than a gourmet burger.

The next day I went to the Athenaeum de la Vigne et du Vin, bought a detailed map of Beaune, and set out with exact instructions from Erik for a loop ride along the Cote d'Or (Slope of Gold). He even wrote to "carefully" cross the D970 into Geanges. The day went swimmingly. I followed the map precisely, rarely looking up from my pannier, making every turn as instructed. This was the wheel world, and in a few hours I was happily back in Beaune. But as we sipped kir royale (a champagnelike sparkling white burgundy blended with black currant liqueur) on the hotel courtyard, surrounded by sculptured Renaissance stone medallions, and compared notes, I found myself with little to say as others described with glee how they got lost in the hills, took wrong turns, and had to retrace enormous inclines and negotiate triple chevrons. Even investment biker Paul (hereafter known as Close-Call Paul) described with stiff-necked delight his fall, in which he skidded out on gravel, trashed his bike, and cracked his helmet. I had nothing to contribute, save a perfect little tour. I never got lost, was never hungry, was on time, and the weather was great. . . . It was all a bit boring.

The following day I set out again on my wheels of fortune with my detailed map and precise instructions and merrily pedaled to the village of St. Romain. Then I did something stupid. Though Erik's map instructed one passage toward Meursault, home of some of the world's finest white wines, I saw a patch of sunflowers down another and decided to take a brief detour. I wound down a lonely road and stopped to admire the rose bushes planted at the end of a vineyard row, and at another spot I picked fresh raspberries. And then, *swiisssh,* and I shuddered to a stop to discover my back tire had gone flat.

Great. I pulled open the repair kit and found a blue plastic wedge to lever out the punctured tube from the frame, but as I worked it round the wheel I suddenly heard a *snap!*—and the wedge tool broke in half.

Really great. Now I was stuck in the middle of French farmland without a farmer in sight with a flat tire. It didn't matter that I couldn't speak French, as there was nobody in sight. The only sound was the wind nagging through my spokes. In an early email describing the trip, Erik had recommended that if anyone got a flat, "walk your bike to a cafe, order a beer, and call a cab." Nice idea, but according to my calculations I was halfway between villages, and the previous one, St. Romain, had nothing open anyway. Above, a buzzard quartered the sky in lazy, graceful curves, its wings barely moving.

Then one of those providential things happened, the kind that only happens when you're lost: A stranger came to help. Seeing my predicament, a bright-eyed Burgundian stopped his Citroën van, inspected my bike, and with a thick farmer's paw made a motion to wait as he drove off. Minutes later he returned and produced a rusted metal version of the wedge, which he immediately jammed into the rim and then expertly pulled off my bad tube.

As I watched the operation I heard birdsong over my shoulder, the first on the trip, and looked up to see a sky as blue as the Gauloises packet my new friend carried. I felt the hot sun on my face. A lizard posed at the edge of the road, looking like a watercolor: art gecko. At last the stranger flashed a sunburst of a smile and presented my bike. The steed was ready to ride. I pulled a wad of francs from my fanny pack and pushed them to my Samaritan, but he furrowed his forehead, put his hands to his chest, palms faced to me, and shook them as his head shook no. With a deep tobacco voice he said, "Bonne route," then motored away, like the Lone Ranger.

Rightly considered, this inconvenience was an adventure, and the kindness of a stranger in a strange land was uplifting. The little tumult was an agreeable quickener of sensation. For the first time I felt unlocked in a way I hadn't in the comfort zone. On guided tours, in taxis, in the back of a car, the world beyond is a blur, and when the pilot gets lost, frustration is the primary response; nothing liberating or fresh comes when a shepherd fails to herd. It is never an internal search that ensues when the person holding your hand takes a turn off beam. And, naturally, when on our own, we try our best to stay on course, to be masters of our fate, captains of our ship. So when once when we err, there is no one to upbraid but ourselves. It triggers a spate of emotions, like Elizabeth Kubler-Ross's stages of death, with the final emotion being surrender, the unmixed acceptance of being lost.

And then, at that most vulnerable point, we suddenly become a vessel for new thoughts, sensations, and perspectives. They pour in as to a tub. We see and sense as never before. Time is stretched as we drink in a magnified beauty, and detail explodes and begins to have meaning. A stranger in another setting is nothing but visual noise. But, when one is lost, a stranger who stops and opens a bag of benevolence is a magician. The world is suddenly enchanted, and anything can happen. I liked the serendipity of getting lost.

On the final day of our bike trip, Erik sketched out a loop that would take us south from the chestnut trees of Puligny-Montrachet through the sleepy hamlets of Remigny, Aluze, and Rully, and then back north through Chagny. The main group had split into three clusters of cyclists. I joined one, but changed my own rules. I left my map and instructions behind, and tooled off in search of *civilization lente* (civilization of slowness). Several times I took the lead and made wrong turns and got lost. But each time, I stopped and looked around and saw the scenery, soaked in the rural beauty, felt the warmth of the breeze, and smelled the *parfum* of baked earth, calla lilies, and lindens. Like a good environmentalist, I often had to recycle the same ground, but with each pass I saw new things. Traveling this way, I regretted the invention of the car. At one point we passed another Tiffany organized tour, and I watched the clients glide by with heads hunkered over their instructions as a beautiful hot-air balloon flew over a field beside them. Even the guide didn't notice, the bland leading the bland. And I pedaled onward, drinking in that youthful feeling of freedom that comes when there are no schedules, no plans, and no routes. After years of guiding European bike trips, Erik really had discovered the best way to ride, the joie de vivre of roving, the art of losing oneself.

Somehow we found our way to Chagny, and to our final *grande bouffe* at the Michelin three-star restaurant, Lameloise (one of only eighteen in all of France). The room was long and elegant; the tablecloth was pulled tight, the cotton napkins double starched, the Baccarat shimmered even in the subdued light. An endless train of waiters, rigid with decorum, came and went on silent feet, and there was a trace of reverence in the air. Erik ordered several bottles of the Bourgogne Blanc Les Setilles from the cellars of Olivier LeFlaive, and we could hear the moist creak of corks being eased from the glassy necks. The menu was so impenetrable that Erik's wife Maryam offered to do an interpretive dance. I was lost among the sprays of the Rabelaisian feast put before me, with such delicacies as *Assiette de Saumons prepares par Nous-Memes Fume, Mi-Cuit et Marine,* and *Sandre dore sur sa Peau Spaghetti aux Herbes a l' Emulsion de Tomates.* I was at sea with the cheese. I was giddy with the parade of desserts that included such yummy delights as *Dentelle Craquante Caramelisee aux Fraises des Bois Feuillete aux*

Poires Caramelisees. I was deliciously lost in a potent but elusive pageantry of gastronomy, and I relished every bite. And I raised a glass of thanks to Erik.

THE ATLAS

ATLAS MOUNTAINS, MORROCO
*Muleteers crossing the Central High Atlas into the Bouguemez
Valley, long a cultivated farmland for Berber herdsmen*

THE ATLAS
Travels with a Mule

From a certain point onward, there is no longer any turning back. That is the point that must be reached.

Kafka

The music of the lutelike oud goes on, a patterned background for our aimless talk. Listening to its notes is like watching the smoke of a wood fire curl and fold in untroubled air. I am with my friend Pam Roberson, a photographer who has spent much of her career in the Middle East, in the restaurant of the Le Tichka Salam Marrakech Hotel, on the northern edge of Marrakech, gateway to the Atlas Mountains. Tired from travel, we linger over the last of our Toulal Guerrouane, a tired Moroccan red wine. Several cats are sprawled around the room in positions that mirror our mood. With muted interest we both look up when the waiter pours a cup of sugared mint tea, deftly cascading the brew from three feet above the table. An idea spills into my head.

"Let's go have tea in the Sahara." I look into Pam's dark eyes, which brighten at the prospect.

It seems a sensible notion, we being so close, though, as always, there is a problem: the great fence of the Atlas Mountains, arcing 1,500 miles from the Atlantic to the Mediterranean, separating the upper body of Africa from the Saharan versant. Created by the same global convulsions that created the Alps and the Himalayas, the perpetually snow-capped Atlas rises to more than

13,000 feet. Certainly we could drive over one of the several passes, but that wouldn't be sporting. Instead we would trek over the soul of the haute range, north to south, to the edge of the famous sands.

The next day at the offices of Atlas Sahara Treks, owner Bernard Fabry unrolls a map on his desk and traces a route with his finger through the Central High Atlas. If we take a four-wheel-drive vehicle we could trundle up the Aroudane Mountain and drop down the other side into the Bouguemez Valley, the end of the road. From there we could trek for four days over the Mgoun massif, breaking on through to the other side. We would eventually reach the Vallee du Dades, where we could hire a vehicle to take us to the oasis of Ouarzazate, "Pearl of the Sands," gateway to the Sahara. Bernard would set us up with a guide from the Bouguemez Valley. "But, I must warn you," Bernard says in his thick latte accent, "the weather this time of year is quite unpredictable. Once in the mountains, if a storm comes in you could be stranded for days, even weeks." It sounds like a plan.

Feeling groggy and guilty for being a few minutes late, Pam and I stumble into the lobby of the Hotel El Andalous at 6:10 A.M. An hour later our guide arrives, along with a new Land Rover Defender. I wonder if perhaps his tardiness is a harbinger of a personality apart from the norm, as guides are generally prideful of their punctuality. He is twenty-two-year-old Rachid Mousklou, who has studied geology for two years at the University of Marrakech and recently, when not guiding, has been teaching other guides about the rocks and birds in the region. He is, apparently, in some demand, as he speaks five languages—English, German, French, Arabic, and his native Berber. He has the glassy black eyes of a doll and a bowed face accentuated by a lack of expression.

Five hours later we are wending our way up the juniper-lined mountain, surging into the snow line. We lunch at the Tizi-n-Tirghist Pass (2,629 feet), then begin the long descent into the Bouguemez Valley. The landscape is denuded, most of the trees long ago felled by the Berber women collecting firewood, though occasionally we pass a replanted grove filled with young black cypress, often topped by magpies, who share the same dull, blackish-gray color as the south side of these mountains.

Our first Berber encounter is in the village of Ifrane, where Mohammed, a friend of Rachid's, bounds out to greet us in his Air Mowabs, a pair of Levis, a fleece jacket, and the same bowed face. He invites us inside for some sweet tea and flinty conversation we can't comprehend.

An hour later we continue our journey to the sole hotel in the valley, the Dar Itarane (House of Stars), in the mud-walled village of Imelghas. It is a lovely and lonely place and, as this is December, we are the only guests. We stake out a spot in the large dining room beneath a cedar ceiling encircled by geometric designs and verses from the Koran, and in front of the fireplace. This will be our base camp.

That evening over oily vegetable soup and lumps of half-cooked lamb fat, Rachid tells us he has been speaking to the villagers and they recommend we don't attempt the Mgoun trek. It is too dangerous this time of year, he says, the weather too unpredictable. He suggests we hike in the other direction, to his father's valley, as an alternative. I unroll the map, trace the intended route for Rachid, and tell him I think we should give it a go. After all, I'd been a professional guide for many years, and if the conditions become too dangerous, we'll simply turn around. "I'm certain we can make it," I tell him in conclusion.

"Inscha'allah," Rachid replies with a shrug before leaving the room for the night.

The sharp morning light fills the room where we slept, the polished floor tiles reflecting the sun on the ceiling as if they were water. After a breakfast of lemongrass tea and bread baked in round, flat loaves from unleavened dough, we decide to explore the valley and stretch our legs before attempting the first pass. We wander among the fields of potatoes, apples, corn, and wheat, and through several of the twenty-five villages in the valley. Rachid is our guide, but for someone so knowledgeable he is surprisingly reticent to share, which baffles me, as generally those attracted to the guiding profession do so because of an inherent love for teaching. He states the obvious, that the valley is sedimentary, my dear Watson, then leads us toward a dramatic knoll, scored with exposed rock that is patterned with swirls like the whorls of a fingerprint.

We scratch our way up the steep hill and wander into a two-hundred-year-old shrine, Sidi Moussa. It is an intriguing piece of architecture, cube-modular, with several tortuous passageways. It has served multiple purposes, Rachid tells me when I ask directly. It has been a watchtower, a winter storage bin, a reliquary, a gravesite for the high and holy and, most importantly, the home of a mountain god, a spirit who not only protects all devotees but also helps to fertilize women. According to legend, a woman who is having problems becoming pregnant must spend the night at Sidi Moussa on three Thursdays in a row. On the fourth Thursday night she must bring an animal to sacrifice, and she will then find herself pregnant.

Back in Marrakech before the journey south, Bernard Fabry had related this myth to me and said he thought there was a more mundane explanation for why those who made the pilgrimage found pregnancy. He told me to notice how similar everyone in the valley looked, and then to take a close look at the face of the caretaker at Sidi Moussa. The caretaker wasn't there, but I did note this was Thursday, and upon mentioning such to Pam, she walks to the altar and gently lays down her multi-colored elastic hair band as an offering to the god, or the eremite caretaker, of Sidi Moussa.

As we walk around the periphery of this belvedere, Rachid looks across the valley to Jbel Waogoulzat, the mountain we are scheduled to climb the next day. It looks like a knee drawn up under a huge sheet. With a staccato gesture he points to a faint stitching in the snow and tells us that is our trail. He grimaces, as though the prospect of the trek is a thoroughly unpleasant one.

We continue our hike to the main village of the valley, Tabant. Next to a former French administrative building is a bar, and outside it a man is sitting on a white plastic chair reading a paper, sipping a cup of tea. It looks very much like a scene outside any Paris cafe, only here the man's face is hidden deep in the recesses of his pointed burnoose, looking like Alec Guinness in *Star Wars*. I wander in, and in front of a blaring television a young child is watching a racy dance number on an Indian version of MTV, and over in the corner a group of teenagers is playing foosball on a set in which the playing field is plastered with the famous nude shot of Marilyn Monroe that appeared in the first issue of *Playboy*.

That evening Rachid sits cross-legged by the fire with a cup of tea in his lap and tells us a story. "There is a superstition in this valley that people sometimes turn into animals. But I think it is more than superstition. My grandmother, who lived to be 110, was transformed into a mule one day. She lived for several more years, but never again as a human."

"Perhaps we should not go into the valley, Mr. Richard," Rachid continues. "The weather does not look good, and I fear something unpleasant could happen."

"Nonsense, Rachid," I snap back. "The weather has been fine, sunny and cloudless. There is no problem with the weather. We'll head out as planned. That's why we're here, and why you've been hired as the guide."

Rachid sulks. He is a stubborn one, and I wonder if the animal transformation thing could be hereditary.

At daybreak we're up and packed, and in the compound is an eagle-faced man named Ahmed and his mule with no name. After he straps our baggage onto the mule, as well as food, cooking materials, and sleeping blankets, we head out. Rachid is in his usual silent mood as we make our way up the trail, which is named The Ambusher. This was one of the caravan passages that carried dates, henna, gold, and salt from the Sahara to the ports in the north, and bands of marauders found this route, with its many overhangs, side canyons, and caves, to be an ideal set for ambushes. Slowly we wind up the pass, through several biblical-looking villages where men with wrapped cloths atop their heads and flowing robes mill about, looking like magi. Up we continue, through groves of juniper, up into the snow, following in the footsteps of our nameless mule. The winter light sifts down from the sky, diffused, slanted, and it gives the landscape a New Mexican look, only here Jane Fonda doesn't own a thing. At one point the mule slips in the snow and almost falls. If the mule were to break a leg he would have to be shot, and Ahmed would lose his greatest ass(et). This would not do, so Ahmed unloads the two largest bags and sets them in the snow. I wonder what his plan is as we continue up the hill, leaving behind two of my bags. It isn't until we are close to the crest that I realize my money, passport, and air tickets are in one of the bags left in the snow, and a nail of panic passes through me. But I'm too exhausted to backtrack.

We crest the Tizi-n-Ait Imi Pass, also known as The Pass of the Sheep with Black Eyes, and are faced with the stunning long, white rooster comb of the Mgoun Ridge across the next valley. Morocco's first invader, the dry wind, howls here, and as I pull on my wool hat, Rachid wraps his head in his *chechia,* his blue Berber head scarf. We all stoop behind a large rock and unpack our lunch: cheese, yellow apples, oily black olives, walnuts, hard-boiled eggs, and bread. While Pam and I nosh, Rachid and Ahmed scramble back down the mountain, returning a few minutes later with our missing bags on their shoulders. Then Rachid points to some clouds in the distance and somberly says, "I think we must go back. The clouds mean bad weather."

But as I survey the sky I see that the clouds are in the north, while the wind is definitely blowing from the south, the direction we're headed. In fact, the sky is a brilliantly blue bowl ahead. "Rachid," I protest, "the clouds are behind us and moving away. The weather looks fine in front. I refuse to be a sheep with blue eyes here. I say we should just keep going. How far to the village where we'll spend the night?"

"Four hours. But we shouldn't go on. It's too dangerous."

What is his hidden agenda, I wonder. I don't believe his weather excuse. I am sorely flummoxed with Rashid and can't fathom what is going on in his impenetrable mind. Why would a guide not want to guide his clients to their target destination?

"I insist. We can do it. There's no reason to turn back," I say, and resolutely I shoulder my pack and start down the trail. With more reluctance than the mule, Rachid follows.

It's an easy descent into the Mgoun Valley, and soon we're walking alongside the crisp Mgoun River. In every direction the view is spectacular and yet daunting, like how I imagine James Hilton's Shangri-la, in his novel *Lost Horizon,* might have been. At one point we pass a series of grottos across the river, with crude wooden ladders leading into the darkness. It looks like one of the Anasazi granaries found in the Four Corners region of the United States. An hour later we pass a fortress, Tighremt-n-Ait Ahmed, which looks like an adobe castle, guarding the confluence of a tributary. Then thirty minutes later we stumble into the Hopi-like village of Talat Righane, where the low, ochre-colored houses seem to have sprung from the ground. We have entered another world. The people here are of the Aitatta tribe, a nomadic Berber confederation that wandered into this valley ages ago and stayed. All the men wear dun-colored burnooses, looking like friars as they sway past us. The women are intricately tattooed with indigo designs on their foreheads and have henna-stained palms and fingers. Pendulum earrings of silver, turquoise, and amber swing as they walk and speak. They wear only black, cornflower blue, and red clothes.

Rachid speaks with one of the village elders, and after a while we're led through a heavy wooden horseshoe-shaped door into a small compound and up the stairs to a narrow room lined with Berber carpets and pillows. This will be our room, he indicates, and brings in a pile of blankets.

After settling in, we step back outside to admire the landscape. It is the moment of twilight when light objects seem unnaturally bright and the others restfully dark. Even in my pile sweater and jacket I still feel the cold like a piece of metal inside me, yet the villagers, in their woolen *djellabas,* don't seem to notice. One woman steps up to Rachid with her small son at her side, and she pulls up his pants leg to reveal a festering wound the size of a half-dollar on his calf.

"What is it?" I ask Rachid.

"A dog bite," he replies with some disdain. There are half a dozen Atlas sheepherder dogs within sight, a couple barking frenetically at our presence.

"Well, isn't there a doctor she can see?"

"Not in this valley. She would have to climb over the pass to where we came from, but she won't because it would take two days and she doesn't want to spend the money for the medicine."

"What about you? I saw you had a medical kit. Can you help?"

"Yes," Rachid said, but the woman and the small boy are already wandering away. "I'll look at the boy before we leave," he says, and turns on his heels to leave the compound. The cold wind blows away the last feeble strands of light.

That night we huddle by a small propane lamp, extracting from it what little warmth it generates. Ahmed brings us tea and *Tajine,* sliced vegetables and pieces of cartilaginous meat cooked over a wood fire, and we chow down. Then Rachid comes in and announces his latest news in his guttural mountain tone: "We can't go on. The villagers say the pass is closed, and it is impossible to proceed." I spit out a tallowy piece of meat with the news.

"Wait a minute. What about the Mgoun River? On the map there is a route that follows the river through a gorge, a route that avoids the pass altogether. Why can't we try that?"

"That, too, is closed. It is impossible to pass this time of year. The water is too high."

"C'mon. This is December. This is the slowest time of year for run-off. We've seen the river; it's low, probably the lowest for the season."

"Well, the river in the gorge is still up to your chest, and the water is too cold now. We can't go on."

"Well, how about we just walk downstream tomorrow and check things out?"

After a long silence Rachid takes a draw on his Casa Sports cigarette, then replies. "Okay, but then we must turn back. You must promise me. We can always visit my father's valley."

Secretly I decide to find someone in this valley with whom I can communicate to get a second opinion. That will be tomorrow's agenda.

But it doesn't work as I hoped. Though I wander around without Rachid's company, but with my phrase books, it becomes apparent that nobody here speaks a word of French, nor Arabic. This is truly an isolated outpost, so much so that the French were never able to penetrate this valley. I don't see a single photograph of King Hassan II, which otherwise appoints virtually every civilized home in the kingdom. Here it is the middle of December, and nobody here, I am certain, has ever heard of Christmas. Somehow I find that delightful, even though I cannot find a soul who can tell me if this journey can be completed.

Finally I begin to hike downstream, in the direction of the gorge, with Rachid at my heels. We pass several Berber women as decorative as any I've seen, festooned with amber necklaces, hair done in the Lily Tomlin operator style. I pull out my camera to take a photo, and Rachid holds his hand up to stop me.

"What's wrong?" I ask.

"They believe you'll be taking their souls; or they'll want money, and that's a bad habit." I can't argue with that, so I tuck my camera away and continue to hike.

Sometime in the early afternoon I heard women's voices raised in song, echoing up the canyon. We are entering the *ksour* of El Mrabitine, where Rachid had said the greatest singers in Morocco lived. Soon we pass the women, who are in a harvest bent, swinging scythes in the fields. They look up as we pass, and I pull out my camera. They smile, and as Rachid is looking the other way, I click a few shots, then press a few dirham notes into the women's hands.

In this Old Testament village there is a single, sand-colored shop, with four men loitering out front, a Berber shop quartet. The store offers the usual items—biscuits, soap, and hard candy—but also a single can of Coke, which I promptly order. Then the shop owner, who has the applelike cheeks of a peasant, closes his shutter and leads us through a labyrinthine set of corridors up to a tea room, where he tears apart green stalks of mint and stuffs them into a little teapot. When Rachid wanders off for a few minutes, I try desperately to communicate with the shop owner, asking about Mgoun Pass and about the river route, drawing pictures in my notebook. But he doesn't understand. When Rachid returns, I close my notebook and take a sip of tea.

"Are you certain we can't go forward?" I implore Rachid one last time, in a voice that rises in a sharp scallop of sound. This exchange is becoming stylized and repetitive, like a belly dance. I suddenly feel a bit foolish with my oft-repeated question. In my twenties I, too, had been a guide, and one of the few unpleasant aspects of the job was dealing with obnoxious clients who repeatedly demanded something impossible. For a second I am horrified to realize that, just as all children become their parents, I was becoming one of my clients.

"It's time to return," Rachid says in a tetchy tone. It is getting late, and since we aren't going forward, we have to leave now to make it back to Talat Righane. But before we depart I step down to the river.

The air is heavy with the odor of spearmint that grows along the banks. I dip my hand in the clear currents. It is glacially cold. The volume has increased with the addition of several tributaries, so much so that it looks like it might be navigated with a kayak or small raft. I find myself wishing I had somehow had the foresight to bring one. Then we could have paddled to the Sahara. I shrug, like Atlas, and turn to head back.

Along the way Rachid breaks his usual silence to tell me he hopes to one day visit the Andes.

"What about Everest?" I ask.

"No," he replies. "The Andes."

Unusual, I think. Every other mountain guide I had ever met dreamed of visiting the Himalayas above all else. But Rachid is like no other guide, a true individualist among a clan of iconoclasts. He has qualities that madden me, but I silently, grudgingly admit to myself that there is a part of me that admires his inimitability.

The following day we stagger back into the House of Stars. The weather has been picture perfect, and I'm bitter and suspicious about whether we could have completed our journey. When I open my camera to change film, I discover that my roll had not advanced, so the photos I took of the Berber women were never captured on film. This main room in the House of Stars, despite a blazing oak fire, seems stuffy and melancholy, full of the sadness that fills a room where disappointment is an occupant. Over couscous Rachid tells me that two Moroccan shepherds died trying to cross Mgoun Pass just last month. He says they started their trek, traveling without mules, and it was a beautiful day. But a sudden storm came in at noon and they froze to death. I don't know whether to believe him or not. The weather has been so ideal, and if we had continued we would at that moment be just one day from completing our crossing.

"By the way," I ask as he's leaving for bed. "Did you ever treat the boy with the dog bite?"

"No," he replies with an absorbed and vacant expression, then disappears. To me, Rachid is a mystery swathed in a puzzle coated in a conundrum. I just cannot understand why he would turn away from a sick boy, especially as a guide, in a profession that is wired for compassion. He is as inscrutable as the skeleton of a mule.

The next morning I awake to the sound of giant trees crashing. But that can't be right, I think blearily, as the few trees here are slight willows and poplars. I realize then it is thunder. My sleep not yet cold, I pull back the shutters. The sky is black and absolute. A huge storm has moved in. It's pouring rain, and lightning streaks across the sky. Fresh snow covers Jbel Waogoulzat, which I can barely make out across the valley. If we had continued, we would have been smack in the middle of the storm.

Rachid was right, his instincts as true as that of the hybrid off-spring of a jackass and a mare, an animal with sagacity, muscular endurance, surefootedness, and legendary stubbornness. Perhaps Rachid is something different than what he appears, something more akin to his grandmother, who wandered though these hills bellowing and braying in her final days.

Four days later Pam and I find ourselves in a 1979 Mercedes 2000D taxi climbing the Tizi-n-Tichka Pass on the way to Ouarzazate, the former slave market at the crossroads of the Draa and Dades Valleys. The weather is still snotty, the storm releasing its last licks. Our driver and guide is Boukhriss A. Majid, a thin, thirty-two-year-old playwright and mountain guide with a salient nose. He is everything Rachid was not: blithe, informative, passionate. He recites poetry and shares history as we wend up through the Atlas the easy way, on the back of a French-paved road. At the crest of the pass, at 7,400 feet, two tour buses had swerved on the ice and now block the way. It looks as though we'll have to turn back, our journey once again thwarted. While waiting by a roadside stand selling red onyx, amethyst, and geodes, a little Berber girl wrapped in a torn shawl plasters me with a snowball and yells through a satisfied smile, "I'm Saddam Hussein; you George Bush." Finally after a couple hours of digging, pushing, yelling, and shoveling sand under the wheels, the buses are liberated and the pass reopens. We coil down through ever-warmer layers of air into a dull rose landscape, past ruined casbahs, past caravans of women, faces seamed with fatigue, bent over double as they carry their loads of firewood. And we pass a mule, back piled high with lumpy, closed sacks, loping down the mountain by itself.

Under a lowering sky we drive through the stout, crenellated walls of the four-star Riad Salam Hotel in Ouarzazate and take a penthouse-type room that sits on the flat roof. From here we can see the sullen sweep of the desert, the date palms, and the shimmering waters of a river that will never see the sea. I check my map and find that the currents of the Mgoun River, which I had touched just a few days before, spill into the Dades, which in turn is a tributary of the Draa River, which flows not far from our hotel. We are reunited. As a white crescent moon begins to swim upward, the waiter brings us our order on an ornate brass tray. And in the soft air we sip hot tea on the edge of the Sahara.

LOMBOK

LOMBOK, INDONESIA
Mount Rinjaini's Segara Anak, the holy crater lake of the indigenous Wektu Telu faith

LOMBOK
The Other Island

T he true paradises are the paradises that we have lost.

Marcel Proust

I first heard of Lombok while watching the 1982 Peter Weir film, *The Year of Living Dangerously,* a romance tale set against the incendiary summer months of 1965 in Indonesia, when communists were plotting a coup, and President Sukarno was about to take his fall. Somewhere in the middle of the film Mel Gibson, playing an Australian foreign correspondent stationed in Jakarta, is praised for a piece he did on Lombok. "I found it a bit melodramatic," Sigourney Weaver taunts, and sets the stage for a steamy passion play between the two characters.

Where is this place, Lombok, I wondered, this island whose decidedly unamorous name helped ignite one of filmdom's epic tropical affairs?

Years later I was in Jakarta, the busy capital of Indonesia, on a business trip, and when I finished early I decided to use the time to head east of Java and explore a fascination. After a consult with a travel agent, I soon found myself eight degrees south of the equator, puttering over the shimmering waters of the Lombok Strait, the deepest stretch of water in the archipelago, in something called a CASA 212. It was a pigeon-white, twenty-four-seater, twin-engine flying shoebox. The nine-minute flight included pieces of hard candy, to help ears pop in the unpressurized cabin, and a stunning approach view of the razor-backed, violently green, mist-wreathed island.

As we touched down at Selaparang Airport (named after a fourteenth-century kingdom), we taxied down a runway whose grassy shoulders were being trimmed by women in big woven toad-stool hats, bent over and wielding tiny hand scythes similar to those used in rice paddies.

After deplaning I climbed into a rusted pick-up truck and trundled up the waringin-tree lined, narrow paved road some ten kilometers north to the Senggigi Beach Hotel, a leading property on the island. The Senggigi Beach Hotel is reason enough to make the trek to Lombok. Opened in April 1987, it is situated on perhaps the most scenic beach in the world. Backdropped by a rim of tropically dressed mountains, camouflaged by groves of coconut palms, it straddles a peninsula of sugar sand and glass-clear water, and looks out due west to the overwhelming majesty of the great volcano, Gunung Agung, 3,140 meters high, and the mother mountain of Bali, just across the way. Every evening, on cue, the sun sets behind this Hollywood matte. A clover-shaped pool, with a sunken swim bar roofed by a replica of a traditional rice barn, is positioned be-tween the open-air lobby and a deer park and aviary, which in turn are just a few steps from the beach. Fragrant frangipani trees hang over the back porches. There are no phones in the rooms (the man-agement will arrange for a wake-up knock on request), but there are mini-bars, air conditioners, and televisions featuring videos at night. It was a comfortable, obscenely scenic retreat, distinctly out of place, the perfect rendezvous site for a Mel and Sigourney tryst.

The following morning a barefoot guide, Surya, took me on a tour of the southern side of Lombok. Surya looked different from the Indonesians on Java or Sumatra. He was darker, his hair was straight, his cheekbones high, and his neck short. He explained he was Sasak, the original and predominate tribe on the island. *Sasak* is the name of a type of bamboo raft once used to cross the Lombok Strait, and legend has it Surya's ancestors arrived on Lombok by these rafts from Burma or northwest India centuries ago, while the lighter-toned people populating the Indonesian islands to the west migrated down the Malay peninsula. Surya explained that, while today virtually all Sasaks are Muslim, originally they were animists who believed in the innate liveliness of inanimate objects.

Sometime in the early 1600s, though, the island was attacked from two fronts. Muslim traders from the Spice Islands established colonies in the east and converted the Sasak aristocracy to Islam, while Hindus from across the Lombok Strait made claims on a western section of the island, a section once used as a penal colony by the sovereigns of Bali. Ruling power passed back and forth between the two religions for almost three centuries, until a Dutch invasion in 1894 officially turned Lombok into a Christian enclave, but not without a bloody fight. When it became certain the superior Dutch forces were going to overpower Lombok, hundreds of resistance fighters, including members of the aristocracy and royal family, committed a ritual mass suicide attack called *Puputan,* in which they deliberately marched into the lethal fire of Dutch artillery.

The Dutch were finally ousted with Indonesia's independence in 1945, and today just 1 percent of Lombok is Christian, another 15 percent is Hindu, and the rest is pretty much Muslim, except for an uncertain percentage, Surya guessed about 3 percent, who practice an odd and unique conglomeration cult called Wektu Telu. It was almost a secret sect, unofficially recognized by the government, and practiced by unknown numbers of peasants in the remote mountains of the north. *Wektu Telu* literally means "three results," and is the consequence of combining the most attractive elements of three religions: Islam, Hinduism, and animism. The fundamental tenet of the faith is that all important aspects of life are underpinned by a trinity: the sun, moon, and stars; Allah, Mohammed, and Adam; the three rice crops their land can produce on a good year. Unlike orthodox Muslims, who pray five times a day, the Wektu Telu bow in prayer on just three occasions: every Friday, the Muslim holy day; on Idul Fitri, the festive day that ends the solemn fasting month of

Ramadan; and on the Prophet Mohammed's birthday. They don't believe in mosques, or any human-made edifices specifically built for worship; they don't practice the haj, the annual trek to Mecca undertaken by Muslims who have both deep faith and pockets; they believe in meditation and their own spirits, some Hindu in origin, others pagan; and they eat pork with impunity. The more I learned about the Wektu Telu, the more fascinated I became. Elements of their peculiar world view fit my own, a cocktail of faiths that idiosyncratically and roguishly extracted only what seemed most desirable. I decided I would make my own pilgrimage to the Wektu Telu.

I asked Surya how I could meet the Wektu Telu, and he explained that their few remaining villages were difficult to reach. Even if we did stumble into one, true Wektu Telu would deny their faith, as government prejudicial policies had turned the religion into an underground congregation. It had formally disappeared in 1968, though everyone knew followers survived in pockets in the high backcountry. Surya suggested the easiest place to encounter the Wektu Telu would be at a sacred hot springs near the top of Mount Rinjani, the 3,726-meter-high volcano that soars over Lombok's landscapes. The Hindus believe the mountain is the abode of Batari, a goddess who battles evil, while the Wektu Telu know that Nenek, a sexless, all-powerful spirit, sits on a cloud-wrapped throne near Rinjani's summit. The Wektu Telu make regular pilgrimages to these hot springs to pray and make homage to Nenek, and if I made the trek as well, I might meet some of the elusive Wektu Telu. I agreed to the plan, and Surya said he would make arrangements so I could make the trek to the sacred hot springs on Rinjani.

Surya spent the next morning shopping for the expedition to Rinjani. When he showed up at the hotel around noon, I asked if there might be anything to see in the lowlands that related to the Wektu Telu or Mount Rinjani. He ushered me to his van, and off we went to Narmada, about twenty kilometers to the southeast. From a distance, Narmada is nothing more than a rise in the road, but once on top of this otherwise ordinary hill an extraordinary sight is presented: a human-made replica of the summit of Mount Rinjani and its crater lake, *Segara Anak* (Son of the Sea). The name *Narmada* comes from a sacred river in India, and the facsimile of Rinjani was built by a Hindu king of Mataram, Anak Agung Gede Karangasem, in 1805, when he was no longer able to climb the real sacred volcano, a variation of Mohammed moving the mountain. Rumor had it the king was a lecherous old man, and he built a hidden viewing room above the artificial lake, where he spent his final days leering at the young girls he invited to come to his court for a swim, a sort of Hindu Hugh Hefner with his version of the glass-walled pool. We were visiting the grounds on a Saturday, and the lake was packed with young maidens, as well as children, boys, fathers, and mothers, out for cool splash and a picnic on a sunny weekend.

Next Surya brought me to *Lingsar* (Running Water), a large temple complex just a few kilometers north of Narmada. In the eighteenth century, Wektu Telu was a much more prevalent, popular, and recognized religion, and in 1714 the Lingsar temple was built with the rather rare concept that two religions could coexist in one house of worship. Thus, Lingsar is designed with two separate sections and levels, with the Hindu Pura on the upper north of the temple, and the Wektu Telu basilica on the lower south.

It was late Saturday afternoon when we rolled to the gate of Lingsar. It was chained and locked, with a menacing etching of Mike Tyson charcoaled across a pillar. Surya poked around, and in an adjacent dwelling found the eighty-three-year-old great-grandmother gatekeeper for the temple, who listened to our plea to see the temple for higher research purposes. She said that would be fine, if we paid her the equivalent of sixty cents U.S.

Inside the inner sanctum we looked first at the Hindu altar, which had a shrine facing Mount Rinjani. Lined in front of the altar were half a dozen basalt stones, carried down from the true summit of the great volcano, wrapped in white cloth and tied with yellow ribbons, a tribute to the Rinjani goddess Batari, who always wears those colors. The Wektu Telu temple was distinguished for its small, enclosed pond, in the shade of a dragon flower tree, devoted to Lord Vishnu. With dainty water lilies floating upon its surface it looked like a wishing well, and in fact silver and gold coins littered its bottom. Surya tapped the walls of the little encased spring and tossed pieces of hard-boiled egg from my lunch box into the clear water. Suddenly, half a dozen fat, sluglike creatures more than four feet long writhed out into the middle of the well and started to nip at the egg pieces.

"Holy mackerel!" I exclaimed at the sight.

"No, holy eels," Surya corrected. These were the sacred eels the Wektu Telu had worshiped for centuries, and farmers to this day make their way off the mountain to come to this place to make offerings and feed the eels who are still a part of their animist cosmology. On the far wall, just beyond the well, was a large-print message in flaring Arabic characters. It was a passage from the Koran, the scripture of Islam.

For the first time I was witnessing the manifestation of this confusing religion. In one holy courtyard all the bases were covered, with tributes to the Hindu god Vishnu, the animist eel gods, and Allah. I covered my bases by tossing three coins in the fountain and making a silent wish for good weather for the next day's climb.

In the pre-dawn dustiness of consciousness I heard the knock. I checked my watch. It was 5:00 A.M., time to go. Benjamin Noya, small-statured freelance Rinjani guide, met me at the door and urged my haste, as it would be a three-hour drive to the starting point for the thirty-kilometer trek. In minutes I tossed my pack into the faded green van and sat back to enjoy the sunrise ride.

Surya was not with us. He had made it clear he didn't cotton to mountain climbing, but in his stead was Ketut Karune, a fine-footed trainee guide who boasted he had prepared for this trek by running five kilometers on the beach last Thursday.

On the ride north, past the black-sand beaches that are testimonies of Rinjani's last eruption, in 1901, Ben gave me a bit of his background. He was a Christian (an oddity on Lombok), one of nine children borne to Protestant parents from the Moluccas, the Spice Islands to the northeast. He had made fifteen successful treks up Rinjani between his continuing studies in economics at the local university. He saw trekking tours as an up-and-coming business opportunity and was saving his rupiah so he could start his own concern. It would be a seasonal affair, as during the monsoons climbing Rinjani is extremely difficult and dangerous. For our trek, in mid-April, the rains were just ending, and this would be Ben's first tour in eight months.

Around half-past eight we rattled up to the end of the road somewhere around six hundred meters above sea level, at Senaro, another traditional Sasak compound consisting of about twenty thatched huts enclosed by a wooden paling fence. As Ketut and I unloaded the van, Ben went off to find porters. Apparently another group had been here the day before and had hired off the first string of porters, so Ben had to go searching in some of the backeddy villages. The plan was that Ketut and I would head up the trail to a lunch-stop shelter and wait there for Ben and the porters.

The hike was up a wide path through a dense forest of mahogany and teak, trees alive with the cascading calls of parrots and lorikeets. An hour into the ascent we stopped in our tracks at the grunt of a wild pig, and looked up to a bolt of white wheeling through the branches. It was, Ketut guessed, a sulfur-crested cockatoo, a bird of Australian origin whose farthest roost west is Lombok, on the edge of the Wallace Line, the demarcation that nineteenth-century naturalist Alfred Russell Wallace drew separating the life forms of Australia and Asia.

A couple hours into the climb, the clouds turned dark, the color of a bruise, and closed in. Then the heavens cut loose, sending down fat columns of rain, turning the trail into a mudslide, mocking my offerings at Lingsar the day before. Bowed and cold to the bone, we slogged along, finally reaching the little shelter around noon. Pulling off our soaked clothes, we discovered leeches with their bloated, rubbery heads buried into our legs, and as we picked them off we shivered violently in the storm. This was not fun, and as I slapped my sides for warmth I wondered about the wisdom of this little exercise. Two hours later Ben trudged up the trail and climbed onto the platform with a worried look on his face. After an extensive search he did at last recruit four porters, but halfway up the trail, one sprained his ankle and had to head back, and the others decided they didn't want to attempt the three-day trek, as the following morning was the beginning of Ramadan, the annual month-long Islamic fast that requires the faithful to abstain from food and water from dawn until dusk. I had been warned not to visit Lombok during Ramadan, the caveat being that the people were cranky and restaurants closed during the fasting hours. The admonition seemed silly to me at the time, but less so now. Ben said he had abandoned our packs down the trail, and had come to tell us the news before heading back down. He confessed he was concerned about finding additional porters, because no one would want to carry heavy loads up the mountain if he couldn't eat or drink.

As I was determined to move forward with my mission, there was little we could do save continue, carrying as much as we could, and trust that Ben could recruit the needed personnel for the rest. Despite all his purported experience, Ben demonstrated little sophistication in packing for the expedition. He had thrown in two cases of bottled water, a dozen heavy tins of meat and vegetables, a jerry can of kerosene, a large stove, various pots and pans, bags of rice, a lantern, and other paraphernalia—so much stuff that it would take four porters to carry it all.

When the rain finally ceased, Ben headed back down the trail, while Ketut and I plowed upward through the muck. Ben was hopeful that he could collect the new porters before sunset and reconnect with us by midnight. Ketut, who had never been in this part of Lombok, was uneasy trekking through the forest with such a small party, and he stopped to strap a knife onto his ankle, just in case we came across any unfriendly Wektu Telu. We reached the base camp hut, near a small artesian spring, at dusk, watched a spectacular sunset across Lombok Strait, then collapsed in sleep, hoping to wake up to Ben and our supplies.

It didn't happen. With daybreak, there was no sign of Ben. After a brief breakfast of cold, glutinous rice, the last of the food we were carrying, we continued upward, up into the mist, stepping up what I now believed was our private stairway to hell. It was now a mission, a goal obsessed, a religious quest, a haj, and I would not turn back.

That all changed when we reached the rim of the caldera, at a vista called Pelawangan, somewhere around 2,600 meters, just above the sailing clouds that snagged on peaks below us. We looked down at a sublime sight, a replica of the scene we'd seen at Narmada, only this time it was the real thing: the revered Segara Anak, the algae-green holy lake. It was much more magnificent than I had imagined, rimmed with pine trees, backdropped by the pyramid summit of Rinjani itself, and punctuated with the black-seamed and pleated cinder cone of Gunung Baru, looking like a spent reactor cooling tower at Three-Mile Island. Segara Anak itself reminded me of Lake Tahoe seen from Heavenly Valley, as it must have been before the casinos and condos. It was easy to see why the Hindus and the Wektu Telu decided this was the throne-room of their mountain gods.

It took three hours to pick our way down the steep inside slopes of the caldera, down to the cold waters of the lake, then around its perimeter to an exit stream named *Kokoq Puteq* (White River) just beneath the leaning, saw-toothed crown of Rinjani. I had been told no fish swam in Segara Anak, but at the source of this stream the waters were boiling with activity, and upon inspection I saw what looked to be dozens of trout dancing in the currents. The sight only reminded me of how hungry I was; Ben still hadn't showed, and he had all the food. Here it was the first day of Ramadan and I was fasting, probably the only Christian on the island to be doing so.

Following the stream a short way, we came to a cliff, over which the water burst in a flash of foam and white then fell twenty meters to a level area spotted with steaming pools. These were the sacred hot springs, our goal, and people were milling about, perhaps the Wektu Telu. I scrambled on down to meet the souls of my quest, but they weren't there. Instead there were European tourists—Swedes, Dutch, Swiss, and German—all here to soak in the scenery and the hot springs. We set up our camp between the Dutch and Swedes, who were in the middle of a clamorous card game, and set out for a bath while we waited for Ben and any Wektu Telu who might show.

The soak was celestial. I found a pool next to the raging stream, just beneath the falls, where I could control the temperature by simply floating toward or away from the cold creek. I laid back in ecstasy, watching a troop of black monkeys across the stream watching me. An hour passed, I think. Time warped in the springs. But at some point Ben and his porters, four Jack Muslims, came over the rise, and I rousted myself out for a much-needed meal, something Ben whipped up that consisted of eggs, asparagus, crab, and hot dogs.

It was sometime before twilight that two dark figures quietly walked into our camp and over to the edge of the river. It was a father and son team, barefoot, with straight black hair. They carried no backpacks, no accoutrements, save a cloth bundle carried like a hobo, on a stick. Ben walked over to my tent and whispered, "Wektu Telu."

I watched as the father and his boy unpacked their prayer rugs, unfurling them on a rock between the foaming river and the springs. As a pair of naked Germans splashed and giggled and soaped up obliviously in the foreground, the Wektu Telu went into a deep meditative trance, called *Bertapa,* and prayed to Nenek, the god of Mount Rinjani.

"Can I speak to the Wektu Telu?" I asked Ben. He advised me not to, for a couple reasons. First, Ben, being a Christian, did not speak their language, and they certainly did not speak English, nor Bahasa, the official Indonesian language. Second, if asked, the Wektu Telu would deny their religion, saying they were simply Muslim. Though they believed in magic and spirits beyond the conventional gods of Islam and Hinduism, they hid those extra theologies from the outside. I asked if they might speak to me if I made an offering. Ben replied that, while they believed in fire-emitting magic swords and flying white horses that rode to the top of Rinjani, they didn't believe in the almighty rupiah, or see value in tourism.

So I kept my distance, and watched the Wektu Telu go through their benedictions. I was impressed, but perhaps for the wrong reasons. They never acknowledged the existence of any of the polyglot tourists who were using their sacred place of worship for a hot-tub party. They never complained, nor intruded. They didn't scrawl graffiti on the rocks. They didn't drop any litter. They never tried to sell us anything. And they never asked for money. They prayed, they spent the night wrapped in thin blankets, and as quietly as they came, they left.

The following evening I was back off the mountain, tired and tempered from the Rinjani experience. It was a sultry night, one that would have quickened the blood of Mel and Sigourney. I wandered across the street from the hotel and found a little *warung* called *Pondok Senggigi* (House of Senggigi). It was packed with young, western tourists wearing sarongs and bright, billowy shirts, drinking beer while a stereo tape-deck alternately played James Taylor and *gamelan,* popular Indonesian music. I looked at the menu and was struck by the prices—they were a tenth those across the street at the Senggigi Beach Hotel—and by the offerings. They ran from traditional dishes, such as Lombok spinach with hot *lombok* (chili) sauce, to cheeseburgers and fries; from *lassis* (liquid yogurt) to papaya milkshakes; from *nasi goring* (traditional fried rice) to freshly trapped lobster. It was confusing, as though the place didn't know what or where it wanted to be, East or West, local or foreign.

As I sat down, a waiter, perhaps a future tour guide, minced over to my table. I looked up and saw he was wearing a tee shirt that read, "Where the Hell is Lombok?" and I thought, nobody, not even the Lombokians, really knows.

THE RIVER
WIRED

Owyhee River, Pacific Northwest, U.S.
Straddling Oregon and Idaho, this beautiful desert river running
between mesas and mud baths offers sunshine and snow to our
Puget Sound rafters. Here, motoring to the take-out.

THE RIVER WIRED
The Secret River

The Spirit of the River laughed for joy that all the beauty of the Earth was gathered to himself.

Zhuangzi (369?–286 B.C.),
Chinese philosopher and
teacher

I blew it. If conditions persisted there would be a mutiny, and I would be drawn and quartered or killed by Indians, I was certain. I had convinced a group of technology executives from Microsoft and Amazon.com (and my old high school buddy, now a neurosurgeon) to join me on a trip down a wild river few had ever heard of. No mention of it even exists in the 108-year-span CD-ROM index of *National Geographic* magazine. I had sent an email invitation describing a high desert river in the extreme southeastern corner of Oregon, one with buttes, mesas, temples, and steep painted gorges reminiscent of the Southwest. It evoked visions of hot, dry air, a welcome respite from one of the wettest winters on record in the Pacific Northwest, and the four-day, mid-May trip filled fast.

The conventional wisdom, though, is that for those with a mind for technology the standard of excellence is a predictable, uniform experience—"The best surprise is no surprise" epistemology promoted by chain hotels, restaurants, and Hawaiian resorts. Most in the technology realm come with engineering backgrounds and as such possess a worldview that all chaos can be ordered, that the environment is like a math problem, binary and deconstructable to a uniform equation. Randomness in nature is just a short-term slip-up, and that all can be ordered and boxed with enough willpower and problem-solving skills. And most technologists live their views, working in standardized cubicles, living in development houses, driving practical cars, wearing sensible shoes. I hoped to show my friends a different side of life—the wilderness, where chaos can't be contained, and there is sheer beauty in the uncontrollable madness of Nature.

Still, even on the eve of departure, my friends wanted to cover every contingency. "What should we bring," was a common phone call, and there seemed to be an expectation of a comprehensive list for every eventuality. "Travel light," I advised. "Bring shorts, tee shirts, a hat, and lots of sunscreen."

Now, here we were ending our first day on the Owyhee River, fifteen miles from the put-in, and we had suffered rain, sleet, hail, high winds, and snow. Nobody was adequately clad. Lee, a pioneer in Internet development, had fallen out of an inflatable kayak into the river and was worried about hypothermia. Those who had hoped to be distracted from the cold by fishing couldn't, as the one store near the put-in that issued permits had been mowed down by an errant truck a couple days before. Now it was late and getting colder, and the shoreline was coated with poison oak. And we had passed all the good campsites, which had been taken by other boaters who already had tents erected and bonfires burning.

At last we were allowed to squeeze into another party's campsite, one co-lead by Everest summiter Pasquale Scaturro. As we huddled around our own fire, sipping tea and trying to thaw out, Pasquale sauntered over puffing a Monte Cristo cigar and carrying a cup of single-malt scotch. He squatted in our circle and pronounced, "Dudes, I can tell you it's colder here than on Everest." I silently remembered the forecast on the Web that had predicted today would be fair, with worse weather ahead. Then, to cap off the evening, another in Pasquale's party, star squash player Caroline

Johnston wandered over to our dying embers and recited the coldest poem ever penned, Robert Service's "The Cremation of Sam McGee." I was sure my friends went to bed wishing I had invited them to Hawaii, not Owyhee.

In fact, the river and its watershed region take their name from the tropic island archipelago. In 1818 the North West Fur Company sent an expedition under Donald McKenzie to explore trade potential west of the Columbia. Upon reaching a steep, unknown river canyon, McKenzie sent three Hawaiians down to look for beaver. They never returned, presumably killed by Indians. The river became known as Owyhee, which is how McKenzie's men heard the doomed islanders refer to their homeland.

Taken as a single piece, this vast network of river canyons and plateaus is the largest undeveloped area in the contiguous United States, and one of the least known. I had heard of the river three decades ago when I was a river guide on the Colorado, sitting around a campfire of guides, swapping one-upmanship tales of exotic rivers—the Snake, Salmon, Rogue, Green, Yampa, Yukon, Selway—but when one guide mentioned the Owyhee, the ring fell silent. Save the one guide, who mesmerized us with tales of labyrinthine canyons and technical rapids, nobody had ever heard of this place. It remained a mystery, even to river cognoscenti.

One reason, I discovered, was the erratic flow of the Owyhee. With no significant dams upstream to regulate flow, the river has no set season and typically just three weeks a year with enough runoff water to allow navigation—and that three-week window could fall anywhere from January to July. This year, though, with the extraordinary snowpack throughout the Northwest, I bet that I could schedule the sixty-seven-mile-long Lower Owyhee River trip in May, and that the basin would be full and the skies blue. Now, only our faces and hands were blue. Wearing every piece of clothing we'd packed, we had launched at about 4,500 feet in elevation in Rome, Oregon. This Rome, a small collection of ranch homes, wasn't built in a day; it looked like it was built before breakfast. And the river corridor was less than impressive, spilling through farm and cattle lands. But as we wound down into a steep-walled basaltic canyon, bouncing through Upset and Bull's Eye rapids, the view got better—not that anyone noticed, as we were hunkered in our coats, flapping limbs to keep warm and dry, longing for climate-controlled cubes.

That night, as I unfurled the official Bureau of Land Management map, I saw that it marked a "hike-out" trail near our camp . . . and I decided to keep the information to myself.

The next day was better. Blasts of cold wind still funneled up the switchback canyon and sleet occasionally coated exposed skin, but there were sun breaks and moments of awe. We meandered past palisades that looked as though they had been hammered into sulfuric slags and ran rapids that shone with incandescence. We passed a fern-encased weeping-wall springs that could have been from the Sandwich Islands and lunched at a trickling hot springs where we took off our wool socks and wiggled our toes in hot mud. We hiked to the ruins of a rustler's cabin, a crumbled address of tuff (compressed white volcanic ash) with a million-dollar view. We watched prairie falcons wheel above as their shadows stained the walls, and we drew the air into our noses to bask in the sweet perfume of sagebrush. We explored Chalk Basin, where a small mountain, banded like a chocolate layer cake, made an appetizing panorama. We purled by gnarled hackberry trees and rabbit brush; by chukars, swifts, and swallows; by a beaver, a water snake, and mother Canada geese with their tiny broods of sea-green chicks. As the day wore on, the winds tempered and the temperature rose. Camp was a real butte, nestled between giant rhyolite bluffs and soaring stone pinnacles. By my tent I ran one hand across a ten-million-year-old piece of volcanic rock, while I touched the petals of a day-old lupine with the other. Time, here, had turned to stone. Back by the cookfire the mood was merry, the group happily playing camp games and sharing tales with scarcely a mention of home, work, or things technologically related.

The following morning dawned with a brilliant sky and the glad songs of red-winged blackbirds. We sailed into a stately black and white vault whose walls were crenellated like a crusader castle. It was an inner gorge as spectacular as any I had seen in half a lifetime of river running, and as the sun burned brighter, clothes were shed, sunscreen was spread, and laughter rang between the walls. We ran the biggest rapids of the trip, Whistling Bird and Montgomery, with just the right mixture of rock and roll, splash and dash, with a hint of danger to salt the brew. We even passed an evocative petroglyph on a riverside rock, a dot within a circle within another circle, divided into eight segments. Probably painted by the nomadic Paiute or Shoshone Indians who hunted here hundreds, perhaps thousands, of years ago, it was ancient art whispering to us from another time.

By late afternoon the baking sun made us lazy, which is the way you are supposed to be on a river. For a time I even rowed with my eyes closed, listening to the descending trill of a canyon wren and the music played by the river's currents.

By the final day the group had succumbed to the seductive beauty of the Owyhee, and blissful grins flashed across the water. My, how things had changed. As I gazed across the piles of resting souls, sprawled across the tubes of the rafts like seals on a beach, I saw sweet surrender. My friends, who live lives trying to tame unpredictability, had laid down their arms (and legs) and were reveling in it. The fact that we had suffered with the cold caprice of Nature early on now made the sunshine and the purling river that much more satisfying.

When, at the take-out at Leslie Gulch, one sunburned high-tech chief said to me, "I would take the Owyhee over Hawaii any time," I knew the river had worked its magic, and that the best surprise was a wilderness untamed, and in the adventure unknown.

THE MIRAGE OF WILDERNESS

THE MIRAGE OF WILDERNESS
Sea Kayaking Newfoundland

O nly to the white man was nature a "wilderness". . . . To us it was tame. Earth was bountiful and we were surrounded with the blessings of the Great Mystery.

Luther Standing Bear

It is impossible not to confront the Janus nature of the island. Its rivers run clean and clear; its air spins with the breath of honeysuckle. Its forbidding interior is a land without litter. Its craggy edges and joints are lodged with deeply religious Protestants and Roman Catholics renowned for their charity and moral excellence. On a sunny day the place seems like heaven. Yet the incessant storms, the frigid waters, have snuffed countless lives, and a pall of violence is forever present. The people here are children of their beloved enemy, the sea. They move with the rhythm of the natural world. Often characterized as optimistic fatalists, they are a thick-skinned and gentle folk who exterminated the Beothuk Indians, hunted a penguin, the great auk, to extinction, and brought the pilot whale to the edge of extinction.

For 450 years the economic mainstay here was a seemingly inexhaustible supply of saltfish. Now the stock has been reduced to a slim fraction of the glory days. Not long ago chief livelihoods included clubbing young seals to death. Presently they include mining, damming wild rivers, and felling trees. Despite these intrusions into its wilderness, few other places survive with such environmental integrity and harmony, yet the urban-based environmentalists of the planet have painted the Rock as a house for eco-bandits, profit-driven types who greedily sacrifice nature for dollars. The island is Newfoundland.

I wasn't looking where I was going. Instead my eyes were sweeping the sky, caught in the sight of seemingly endless skeins and clouds of flickering pinions. It was a world of wings, millions of them, arrow-swift murres, Pillsbury dough-bird puffins with their clown-colored beaks, great-winged gannets flying arabesques betwixt and between until the sky seemed alive with flight. I continued to paddle as I ogled the phalanxes, until suddenly I heard a *thud*.

It was not more than a tap, really, with the force I imagined a Newfie sealer used when clubbing the nose of a whitecoat. Looking down I saw I had bumped broadside into Gerald's kayak, and my heart sank as I saw him teeter back and forth, and then in a slow-motion roll, he poured into the deep indigo-blue waters of the icy North Atlantic.

The words of our guide suddenly spun with my paddle: "A person can only function for five minutes in this water; then he goes numb, helpless." I positioned my kayak next to Gerald and reached to him as he grabbed the edge of my boat, almost turning it over in panic. This wasn't right, I thought, and rocked my hips to maintain balance. We were both saved with the command from our guide Jim: "Richard, move out of the way." I dug a few strokes toward the spume of a humpback whale several hundred yards away, but pulled my eyes back around to watch as Jim and his protégé, Young Doug, with cool, quick professionalism, line up on either side of the overturned kayak. Placing a paddle between the upright kayaks as a brace, they pulled Gerald's boat from the water, drained it, flipped it over, and positioned it in the water between them. Then Jim instructed Gerald to pull himself on board as the guides stabilized his craft. In four and a half minutes Gerald was back on board, the rescue a memory of finesse, and we all continued our paddle to Great Island.

Those who live here call it The Rock or the Granite Planet. The explorer Jacques Cartier christened it "the land God gave to Cain." None does it justice. A garden of wildflowers, a sanctuary for moose and caribou, host to the greatest fish pastures in the world, a landscape of tall trees and hard splendor, Newfoundland is much more than a slate stopper thrust into the bell-mouth of the Gulf of St. Lawrence. It is the tenth largest island in the world. More than a thousand miles northeast of New York, it is the most easterly land in North America. It turns its back upon the Canadian mainland, barricading itself behind the three-hundred-mile-long rampart that forms a western coast as tattered as an old fishing net. Its other coasts all face the grim ocean, and are so slashed and convoluted that they present more than five thousand miles to the sweep of the "Big Pond," a favored Newfie name for the Atlantic.

Newfoundland is of the sea, and so I felt there could be no better way to explore the narrow gaps bitten in its foreshore—its coves, bights, inlets, reaches, runs, and fjords—than by sea kayak. I found myself with Eastern Edge Outfitters, traveling through the glacially scoured scapes that define an old land that some insist has yet to be found.

Traveling with photographer Pamela Roberson, our week-long sojourn started on Friday the thirteenth at Lower Lance Cove on Random Island, off the serrated southeastern coast of Newfoundland. The first thing Jim Price, our guide, did was go through our gear and winnow out 75 percent to be left behind. "This is not a cruise or a raft trip," he said, his eyes crinkling at the corners as he spoke. Besides, as I later discovered, he wanted as much premium space as possible to pack his wife Margie's cooking, and for good reason.

When I was properly shaken down to a single change of clothes, I slipped on my sprayskirt (backwards at first) and slid into the percussively sleek twenty-foot blue-and-white fiberglass tandem kayak. This craft has come a long way from the driftwood and animal-skin version devised by Eskimos four hundred years ago. I would be sharing the boat with Pamela, the photographer for our expedition. This was my first time in such a craft, and for the first few minutes I felt like a goose among swans. Finally, though, I got my sea legs and arms and we were off, the bow shedding waves as we paddled east down Smith Sound toward the North Atlantic.

The boat was remarkably stable yet agile, cutting through the water like a slim missile, and after an hour I felt as though I'd been born into this boat. The vexations of the urban, managed world washed away with the water that fell from my paddle blades, and I expanded my chest in the big, cold freedom of salty air.

The scenery was exquisite. We cruised along a ripsaw coastline marked with black spruce, stunted fir, and gaunt, granite walls, past the occasional lobster pot. Arctic terns by the hundreds sailed their sharp chevron wings above us. A tiger swallowtail, Newfoundland's largest butterfly, fluttered across the bow. After a few leisurely hours we turned around a barb in the land, Hayden Point (after the captain who wrecked his schooner here), and paddled into a small, protected bay called Gabriel Cove. We were at Thoroughfare, a once busy outport, now abandoned because of government relocation policies. All that remained was a pelt of tawny grass swept with wild irises, purple lupines, tall meadow-rue, marsh marigolds, daisies, and buttercups.

Thoroughfare was one of 148 communities in the Random Island area resettled in the 1960s by the government, in an effort to centralize population in "growth centers" where public services, such as transportation, schools, and medical care could more readily be provided, and the island could be recast into an industrialized principality. More than twenty thousand people were promised new jobs and a better life as they were coerced to move as part of this program that saw Newfoundland turning its back on the ocean and becoming a manufacturing and services center, more like Chicago than a string of fishing outposts. By and large the jobs were made of air and sea foam—the government was not able to make its visions real—and the proffered new life was one of psychic and spiritual havoc.

We set up shop, then hiked into the birch and tuckamore to the ruins of a once-active merchant post that served the "thoroughfare" tickle through which boats traveled to and from Smith Sound. Today, picking through the planks and woodchips, we could identify just two former structures: the town sawmill and the steeple of the church. After the little archaeological dig we washed and collected soft water from the little spring that trickled down an alcove just across the inlet from our campfire, and after a dinner of fresh salmon and cod tongues fried in batter we made an early retreat to bed.

The next morning, after a nursery-colored sunrise and the alarm clock of a robin singing near my tent, we sat down to a breakfast of fried pancakes, sausage, and thick coffee. With a second helping, we looked up to see what appeared to be a black-bearded pirate approaching in a white kayak. It was Mark Dykeman, Jim's partner, just in time for the second pot of coffee. Working as a construction manager in St. John's, he could only take the weekend off, so he had left at 4:00 A.M. this Saturday and kayaked the nine miles to meet us for breakfast.

By midmorning, under a sky that foretold rain, we were off and paddling across the tickle toward another, smaller island, Ireland's Eye. To get there we had to leave our protected cove and round an exposed stretch of the island, a stretch lashed by the waters of Trinity Bay. For a moment I felt we had dialed back a thousand years and were part of that small band of Norse explorers steering high-prowed longboats up to the New Founde Land. But my Viking fantasy lasted a brief moment.

Just as we broached the rolling waves, my feet slipped off the pedals controlling the rudder. I squirmed around inside the boat, trying to reposition legs and feet, but couldn't make the purchase. A wave of panic rolled over me, and Pamela began to yell at Jim, who was paddling merrily along a few hundred yards ahead. After several screams and some frantic paddle waving, he saw us and sprinted back to our bobbing boat, which had turned into the wind and was weathercocking. In a flash he ripped off my sprayskirt, reached into the bulkhead, readjusted my rudder pedals, and resealed my skirt. His face wrinkled up in a cocky grin as he motioned we should follow, and off we went.

After a few miles we turned into the snug harbor that once served the town of Ireland's Eye. It was called such because a hole in a rock in the bay faced toward the Emerald Isle, and legend held that on a clear day a viewer could spy the ancestral home through the hole.

Negotiating this harbor, it appeared we were paddling into the seventeenth century, which is when the town first appeared on maps. Big chimney-potted clapboard houses with mansard roofs and curved dormers perched above the cliffs on both sides. Directly in front of us, at the end of the bay, stood a large, white, wooden neo-Gothic Anglican church. But the windows had no eyes here; the pews gave no songs. Ireland's Eye is a ghost town now. The only living creature we saw was a great bald eagle, who swooped over us, glowering with amber eyes, signaling, it seemed, that he was now the mayor and constituency of Ireland's Eye.

The day turned mauzy. We parked in front of a blossoming lilac tree, and under an oblique rain Jim brewed a pot of tea and cooked up a pithy stew packed with pieces of a moose he had shot months before. After a dessert of Margie's cookies (the best I've ever tasted; I wished I'd left even more gear behind to make more room for Margie's baked delights), we trudged up a dripping-wet, overgrown path across a landscape that seemed to have risen overnight from the sea, to explore the burg of Ireland's Eye.

The town is most famous for its drug bust. In August 1988, local fisherman, suspicious of high-speed boats zipping in and out of Ireland's Eye, called the Mounties, and Canada's largest hash bust took place. Sixteen tons, with a street value of $200 million Canadian dollars, had been stashed inside the cavernous church, which is where we now stood, admiring the hand-crafted chancel and apse and wondering how it could ever have been forsaken.

We hiked back behind the church a few hundred yards

through a thick alder grove and stepped through a spindly white fence to the graveyard. Woodland mushrooms lined the raised edges of the graves. The tombstones, slanted from the settling soil, were decorous affairs, carved in white marble, and I could clearly read inscriptions that told of people born more than two centuries ago: "Edward Cooper, died May 6, 1868 at the age of 87." I wondered of his life and of life in his time, and guessed it was little different a hundred years later when his relatives were compelled to relocate and abandon their heritage.

That evening, after a dinner of fresh mussels, Newfie steak (fried baloney), onions, and baked potatoes, Jim changed to his roll-necked Guernsey and pulled from his haversack a bottle of Screech, an imported Jamaican rum so named for the reaction its potency tends to produce. After a few swigs, Jim and Mark loosened up a bit and told a little of why they entered the outfitting biz. Jim insisted it was "just for the halibut," while Mark confessed his goal was to someday turn outfitting into a full-time profession, though for now the motto of their tiny company was, "Don't quit your day job." Both were keen kayakers, and had met seven years ago boating some of Newfoundland's wild rivers. They continued to spend weekends and vacations together exploring new waterways, and once even kayaked to France. Well, they kayaked the fourteen miles to St. Pierre, the French territory just off the bony Burin Peninsula, a southern finger of the hand-shaped island. Now, both in their mid-forties, they've decided to see if they can make a business as one of a handful of adventure tour operators on the island, and we were members of one of their first commercial tours.

On the way back from Ireland's Eye, Pamela's eye noticed a moving brown speck on shore. We paddled closer, and the fuzzy shape sharpened to a distinct form: a young moose. It was one of the seventy thousand or so that now roam Newfoundland, a non-indigenous species introduced to the islands in 1878. It didn't acknowledge our presence and continued to munch on partridgeberries, even as we parked the kayaks on shore just a few yards from his lunch spread. It was only when Pamela stepped on shore to get a close-up shot that the moose decided to move back into the boreal forest, back into the interior to places still unknown to humans.

The sun shimmered as though dipped in a bowl of crystal as we packed the following day. It was a grueling five-hour return paddle to Lower Lance Cove. When at last we pulled our boats on shore, we met two plucky white-haired women, Blanche Ivany and her cousin, Martha Stone. In a burr rich as Irish cream they told me why they were there. Blanche, a widower, was born in Ireland's Eye in a four-square, two-story house in 1931, and lived there with her fisherman husband, Lambert, until 1963. Then the government withdrew funds for the post office, the school, and the government store, and residents were inveigled to move. She and her husband were given nothing for their land or home; just $600 in expenses to reestablish within Trinity Bay. But once moved they could find no work, so Lambert would use his dory to make the long trip back to his old fishing grounds at Ireland's Eye. He died, she said, in 1987, at the age of sixty-one, of a broken heart. Now, every Sunday she and her cousin, who was also a victim of relocation, come down to the shale beach at Lower Lance Cove and look across the water toward their old home.

The next day we were paddling off the windswept eastern coast of the Avalon Peninsula, as far east as a paddler can get and still be in North American waters. We were in the Witless Bay Ecological Reserve, on our way to Great Island, one of the world's largest puffin rookeries, when I bumped into Gerald's kayak sending him into the brink. Gerald took it all in stride, but I couldn't help but feel he hoped for some sort of revenge. It came minutes later, as we paused in a clangorous cove at Great Island to gawk at the wheeling masses of beer-bellied puffins, black-legged kittiwakes, stubby-winged guillemots, cannon murres, and yellow-headed gannets, Newfoundland's largest sea birds. I had never seen such a sight, the sky blazed with wings, and as I looked skyward I inadvertently opened my mouth in awe, and immediately felt something foreign drop in. It was bad enough to think of what had happened, but I hate anchovies, and could tell that's what my bombardier ate for breakfast. As I spat and wiped myself clean, Gerald's laughter rose above the squawks of the fowls of the air, as though he knew the gods were just evening the score.

After circumnavigating the much-guanoed Great Island, poking into a sea-carved cave Jim nicknamed the Dragon's Throat for its esophageal rumblings, and running through a natural sea arch, we paddled back to the mainland, toward the town of La Manche, another abandoned outport, but this time not because of political gerrymandering, although there had also been government pressure to move. In January 1966, a tidal wave washed away all the boats and stores of La Manche, and most of the homes. It was as though God was siding with the government, and so the residents of La Manche capitulated and agreed to be resettled.

We actually beached, however, at the wharf at nearby Bauling East, an active fishing community with a knot of confetti-colored houses. Leaving the protected bird sanctuary behind, I paddled with a feeling that Newfoundland was perhaps now sailing with an environmental tact. But as we pulled our boats onto the dock, I couldn't help but notice a stench mingled with the iodine tang of kelp. Dozens of dead puffins, their already dumpy figures looking even more bloated, were floating in the tidewash. They weren't the victims of insecticides, oil spills, or poaching. Rather, they were the result of cod fishermen's dragnets, which are spread over such a distance that when hauled in they invariably capture a few of the puffins floating on the surface.

For the final leg of our kayak exploration, we moved to the other side of Newfoundland, to the 450,000-acre Gros Morne (Big Gloomy) National Park, on the primordial coast of the Gulf of St. Lawrence. Named a UNESCO World Heritage site in 1988, the park has been called the "Galapagos of plate tectonics" because of its exposed expanses of the earth's mantle that shows various stages of the earth's evolutionary history. The park also showcases Newfoundland's land conservation policies: Here is an extraordinary wilderness where moose, caribou, and black bear can wander completely protected, and people can explore a backcountry without crowds or trash bins.

The park is even willing to trial balloon new policies that could help maintain the park at a savings to the government. Before getting back in our kayaks, we took a hike up one of the park's more popular trails to Berry Hill, a rock knob that was an island during higher sea levels just after the last ice age. At the trailhead was a deep box filled with gravel, and a sign inviting us to participate in "an experiment in reducing costs while maintaining quality." Then it gave directions, asking hikers to fill the can with gravel, carry it to the top of the hill overlooking the park, spread the gravel on the trail as an erosion preventative, and then return the can at the end of the hike. It was an idea brilliant in its simplicity. The only problem was there was no can; it had been stolen.

It was a two-mile peat-bog trek to the put-in at Western Brook Pond. Along the way we passed several insect-eating pitcher plants, the somehow appropriate provincial flower. Once there, the clouds darkened, the wind began to wail, and the water whipped itself into whitecaps. This did not look like pleasant paddling weather, and even Young Doug, who had recently placed seventh in the flatwater kayaking competition in the Canadian Games, wondered aloud if the "white horses" (whitecaps) might be too rough for our planned trip. But Jim, fearless as a snake charmer, would hear nothing of it. Bubbling with his boyish optimism (a result of Margie's cooking, I was certain), he had us launch and begin paddling against the cutting wind up the famous pond.

Western Brook Pond is not really a pond. In typical Newfie understatement, most any lake or large body of water is called a pond. "To a Newfie, a lake is a hole in your boot," Jim told me. But this was more of a rock-girt fjord, looking like something out of Norway or New Zealand. Ultimately it didn't matter what you called it—pond, fjord, lake—at that moment it was a combing sea of spindrift, and

I was paddling in fear of a capsize. Yet, as I paddled toward its gates, mind fogged in fear, I couldn't help but look up and be stunned by the scenery. The cleft in the mountains ahead looked as though it had been split clean by a giant axe. It was like paddling into a flooded Yosemite Valley, one with no hotels, no galleries, no Laundromats, no tourists. Just rearing, glacially scrubbed granite cliffs, 2,200 feet high, beckoning, and I responded, not just for the view, but because between those protected cliffs I could see the water was a lot calmer.

An hour later I pulled off my poogies (elbow-long neoprene gloves); we were in the sheltering arms of the beetling cliffs, the wind now at our backs, and the water, while not Formica smooth, was at least forgiving. From here the ride was a pure delight. I even tried sailing, furling my lifejacket between the blades of two paddles, but the irregular wind made it a tricky and tiring endeavor, so I abandoned the technique for more traditional locomotion. We passed the dramatic spill of Blue Denim Falls on the left and gneiss hanging valleys on the right. Then Wood Pond Falls on the left, a cascade falling more than 1,500 feet. The dark color of the water beneath us was an indicator of its depth, some 540 feet, and the water was arctic cold, forty-nine degrees Fahrenheit. On the right, with a squint, we could see the red granite seams in the face of an ancient mariner etched in the cliff top—a very old man indeed, probably around 600 million years old, if the geologists are correct. We stopped at a rookery of great black-backed and herring gulls, perched saucily on the cliffs and taking flight as they scolded us for disturbing their day. I was careful to keep my mouth shut while admiring their aerobatics. Then with a few more strokes the canyon made a scimitar turn and we were faced with the piece de resistance of the park, Pissing Mare Falls, the longest and most spectacular falls in Canada, dropping 1,850 feet from the canyon rim.

After ten miles of paddling we pulled onto the pebble beach at the west end of Western Brook Pond. Not surprising, we were the only campers in this quasi-paradise. "Quasi" because though the beauty was nonpareil, the experience was a bit tainted by the black flies—thousands of the pesky biters, always ready for a piece of exposed skin or a ready orifice. But we discovered the cure: Screech, in large doses, taken internally. After a few applications we didn't feel a thing, until the next morning.

It was late morning by the time we started up the trail. The plan was to hike to the rim of Western Brook Pond, where one of the grandest (and least seen) vistas in all Newfoundland could be savored, and then return in time to kayak back before dark.

I decided to start out ahead of the others so I would have time to take photos. This was unlike any trail in any national park I had ever seen. A rotting hand-carved sign pointed westward, the wrong way, from our campsite, with the simple designation, "Trail." It would be the last sign, sure or otherwise, of our whereabouts. Just a few yards from camp the path vanished in the spongy tuckamore, but it wasn't cause for alarm as there could only be one way to go— up the U-shaped valley toward the Precambrian walls of the Long Range Mountains, the northernmost extent of the Appalachians. Behind was the pond, and on either side the sheer walls, sharp and sudden as the side of a box, defied negotiation. So, swatting through the brush, climbing up the boulders, wading through the muskeg, I continued upward.

It was an intoxicating hike. Waterfalls materialized out of riven rock, and the views became grander with every step. This was July, yet patches of snow lit up the gray fans of scree in cirques. Then after a couple of hours scrambling up a recent rockslide, I was faced with a decision. To the left was a side canyon that looked as though it offered a passage to the top. The alternative was to drop back down a saddle into a second streambed and climb up the other side of the main canyon to a slope that appeared gentle enough for a summit attempt. I chose the closer route, the left ravine, and began my assault.

It was quickly apparent I was on the wrong route. The vegetation became denser; there was no way to move forward save to claw upward, swimming upstream in a river of birch and springy juniper. It was grueling, sweaty work, but I gritted and kept going, feeling it the wisest course, believing I would be above the tree line soon, and then just a dash away from the top.

After an hour of hand-to-hand combat with the goblin forest, of scratching through a tangle of larch and alder, I emerged above the tree line onto a glacial drumlin and surveyed the landscape. It didn't look good. The gully I had hoped to scale narrowed into a dark chimney, and the final pitch of a hundred feet or so was slippery and sheer, impossible to traverse without ropes and pitons. I had successfully climbed to a dead end.

Then I heard Jim's voice echoing from across the canyon: "Where are you?" I yelled back, and thought I could see a rustle of trees about a mile down the abrupt valley.

"Come down!" Pamela's voice now reverberated. But I was exhausted and needed a few moments before I could move, so I sat down on a lichen-covered rock and pulled a Mirage chocolate bar from my pocket. As I unwrapped it I looked back down the valley for the first time in a couple hours, and was stunned by the sight. Some blessings, I knew, came from Nature, unbidden and unplanned, and this view was one. I imagined it the sort of landscape the Maritime Archaic people who made their way here along the edge of retreating glaciers ten thousand years ago must have beheld. To my left was the misty veil of the great falls, and above, a bald plateau where I could make out a small herd of barren ground caribou cooling off on a snow patch. I could gaze all the way to the end of the snaking Pond, and beyond to the Gulf of St. Lawrence, the waters infamous as the killing fields for millions of baby seals. It was tranquil now, deep blue, no sign of the red tide, the blood of countless seals that so recently stained these waters. And as I sat there watching a scene of unmitigated calm, I munched my Mirage bar and reviewed the lineaments of this odd island. When I finished the candy, I bunched up the wrapper and began to stuff it in my pocket.

Then I stopped, balled the wrapper tighter, and tossed it against the cliff. Somehow it seemed the thing to do, like Ed Abbey's insistence on throwing beer cans along the highways that dissected his sacrosanct desert landscapes. But this wasn't out of anger. It was to defy the immutable morality of the environmentalists who had never visited this place, but had so heartily condemned it—through public rhetoric, boycotts, and disinformation. I knew the simple act of leaving trash in a wilderness would incur the wrath of anyone with green leanings, and I counted myself in that troop, yet in this case it didn't warrant it, or so I rationalized. I was probably the first human to ever stand on this perch. Even the Beothuk Indians were too smart to have tried this route, and likely no other human would for many years to come. By that time the rain and storms and severe climate would have long obliterated the paper wrapper. If a wrapper is left where nobody ever sees it, is that trash? Perhaps. But the small act also seemed in some way to express my frustrations with the ecological invective hurled at this island and its people.

There seemed a singular cohesiveness of culture and society here—fisherpeople, people who share the sea. If the traits worn on the sleeve of Jim Price represented the Newfie character, I then deeply admired these folks: After paddling with him, I esteemed his self-sufficiency, adaptability, daring, endurance, unbounded hospitality, appreciation of wilderness, and evergreen good will. The history of the people here is one of exploitation, of interference in the modest goals of feeding and sustaining a healthy family. For centuries they caught or killed what the biblical Great Waters offered as their currency with the world—seals, whales, and codfish—but then the world turned against them, condemning the hunting of seals and whales.

Simultaneously, foreigners were employing high-tech vessels with sophisticated radar to beat them in the fishing game. In 1986, when Spain and Portugal joined the European community, they blithely ignored the voluntary fishing allocations and every year have taken five times their quota from the shallow waters just beyond the two-hundred-mile Canadian limits. The fall in fish stocks has forced the Canadian government to cut its own quotas by enough to throw three thousand Newfoundlanders out of work, and scientists insist quotas will have to be cut far more deeply if stocks are to revive. This in a province where the official unemployment rate is 17 percent (privately, some told me it was in fact closer to 30 percent), the sales tax is an ungodly 12 percent, and incomes are only two-thirds the Canadian average. In recent years many former sealers, whalers, and fishermen turned to logging, but now a vocal band of outsiders is again jeering the destruction of a limited resource, organizing boycotts and fighting for legislation that would halt these practices. Now everything seems to be running short except hard luck stories.

Nonetheless, the resourceful are turning to new sources of income. I couldn't help but notice on my journey that the island's highways are lined with cheap motels, gas, bars, waterslide parks (when there are less than sixty hot swimming days a year), and tacky tourist shops selling mock cans of Moose, ceramic Newfoundland dog decanters "produced entirely by local craftspeople," lobster parts glued together to look like fishermen, and "In Cod We Trust" posters—Newfoundland in a can. In 1988 the government invested more than $17 million Canadian in a cucumber greenhouse scheme that quickly went bust. And while I was there the Economic Recovery Commission announced it was going to invest in an ice factory for the exportation of Newfoundland ice. And then Jim and Mark have their kayaking ventures.

There is no pat answer. As components of a vulnerable living fabric, we cannot allow the destruction of any species, but it is too bad the human side of the issues are rarely adequately addressed. Greenpeace, Bridgitte Bardot (who made a well-publicized trip to an ice floe in 1977 to protest against the annual seal pup hunt), and animal-rights author Farley Mowat ("Hardly Knowit" is a favorite nickname here) are practically national enemies in Newfoundland; they've portrayed the good people of The Rock as biocidal Darth

Vadars, when in fact they are decent and in many ways extraordinary folks simply trying to eke out an existence in ways that were honorable just a few years ago. The key is to find viable alternatives, and the environmental groups would do better to back off the personal censure and castigation and instead work with the Newfoundlanders to build a better life, something beyond the Rod and Gun Waterslide Park.

I took one last gaze at the Mirage wrapper, reweighing my decision. Yes, I would leave it behind. Then a gust flew across my shoulder, picked up the wrapper, and sent it sailing into a pine tree. Soon after another cold current funneled up the canyon, slapping my face, which had been sweating from the reflected July sun. It was a tingly combination of hot and cold, like a Baked Alaska. A storm was on its way. I buttoned my coat, turned, and began the long slog back down the mountain.

Three hours later we were recongregated at camp, battening down the hatches. A squall had grabbed my Eureka tent and tossed it into the hemlocks, and other bits of raiment and light gear were scattered with the wind. The waterfall above us was actually being blown upward, so the water seemed to be running upside-down. On the plus side, even the black flies had been blown away. The pond that looked so composed just a few hours earlier was now a stark and wild inebriate.

"We've got gale force winds; we can't kayak. We're stuck," Jim announced in a sober tone that was completely unfamiliar to us up to this point. It looked as though we would have to hunker down for the night and wait out the storm, when around the bend appeared the Westbrook 1, the forty-two-foot-long skiff that regularly carries tourists up to the far end of Western Brook Pond. Pamela took out a white windbreaker, attached it to the top of her paddle, and waved at the tour boat.

Skipper Charles Reid steered his pitching vessel toward our encampment, then announced over his loudspeaker that it was too rough; he couldn't make it in; we were on our own. It was daunting news, but then the russet-faced skipper turned the boat around and somehow backed into our little cove. Quickly we threw on our kayaks and camping gear and were soon sailing back to safety at the eastern end of the pond.

As the Westbrook 1 cruised amidst the skirling wind and waterspouts, I climbed topside to take a last look at this uncommon landscape. The canyon was filled with blue tendrils of fog and cold water sprayed across my glasses, but for a moment the mist cleared and the sun shone through, lighting up the brooding cliffs and the grand falls, turning its spray into a brilliantly wavering spectrum of color. It was a magic moment, and I couldn't but think that the entire scene looked like a mirage.

UP AGAINST THE WHALING WALL

INSIDE PASSAGE, BRITISH COLUMBIA, CANADA
Paddling through the thick fog of Johnstone Strait, between Vancouver Island and Vancouver, B.C., renowned as the most populous body of water for sighting Orca pods

UP AGAINST THE WHALING WALL
Paddling the Passage Inside

> Though once there were more whales cast up
> here, I think that it was never more wild than now.
>
> **Henry David Thoreau**

"Tons of whales. Out in full parade. August is the best time to see them. It's a festival of nature!" His words splash like clear brandy in a snifter. It is the day before departure, and I've called David Arcese to ask about gum boots, an unfamiliar item recommended as en route footwear. David, however, is so excited by the upcoming trip he can't stop speaking about the whales: *Orcinus orcas,* blackfish, killer whales, the residents of the glacially carved channel where we will be kayaking for a near week.

And so it is we are going to paddle among the orcas. There is no better place, no better time. The salmon are running, and the weather is fine. Our target waters have the highest density of orcas anywhere in the world. I'm convinced I'm going to feel the spray of flying flukes, and wink at the melon-sized eye of an orca.

Monday morning we depart from the Haida-Way Motel in Port McNeill, where a taxi takes us twenty minutes down the coast to Telegraph Cove, a museum piece of a fishing village on the northern edge of Vancouver Island in British Columbia. Here we find living testimony to the booming popularity of sea kayaking: On the lawn of a bustling tackle shop, dozens of sea kayaks are strewn in various states of readiness, including those for a group that will be paralleling our itinerary, "The Other Pod," as we inventively tag them.

There are four fiberglass kayaks for our expedition: three twenty-one-foot doubles and one seventeen-foot single piloted by David Arcese, forty-four, owner of Northern Lights, our outfitter. Five-months pregnant photographer Pamela Roberson will occupy the bow of my jellybean-green vessel; in the ocean-blue one we find Alison, the CEO of Patagonia, the outdoor clothing manufacturer, and her brother Jon, who has the Radio Shack franchise for Santiago, Chile. In the red-tide version: Wendy, David's girlfriend, a speech therapist from southern California whom he met on a kayak trip last season, and Marlene, partner in a Reno, Nevada marketing firm. Everyone is wearing gum boots, heavy black knee-high rubber galoshes, except Wendy, who sports an electric-blue pair of disco boots, a fashion statement from the Jetsons; and me. Though I bought the suggested footgear, the day seems too warm, so I stay in my Tevas, sandal-wear from my rafting days.

We slip on our spray skirts, wiggle into the boats, and off we sail into water the serving temperature of Chenin Blanc. Our route is down Johnstone Strait on the Inside Passage, a stretch of water famous for its accommodating orcas. Beyond the dorsal fins, we'll admire the sublime scenery along the Vancouver Island coast. Then, after paddling southeast for about six miles, we'll camp front-row at a favorite spot for sighting big saddle-patched cetaceans.

The going is slow the first hour. Still getting our sea arms, we drive our boats in wild directions, bumping gunwales, sometimes pointing at four compass points, other times facing one another like wrestlers. Kayaking is a lean, clean, aerobicized form of boating, and a bad paddle stroke is like a thong bikini, exposing all structural flaws. I had been a rafter for many years, and at times want to cover my pear-shaped fumblings in the loose old bathrobe of a big rubber inflatable. But after a time I get the hang of it, and can't help but appreciate the beauty of the bright lines the boat carves in the water as we charge forward. Now I can look up and see how beautiful the shoreline is as well, looking like an enormous green animal in repose, though occasionally great brown chevrons of slash scar the shoulders, giving the odd impression that the creature is molting.

As happens, this is one of the few days of summer commercial fishermen are allowed to catch salmon, so the strait is crammed with diesel-powered trawlers, and we have to dodge them and their nets, our subtle crafts murmuring past their obtrusive presence. Then I hear it . . . the eerie, low wailing sound of a whale. There must be one nearby. It calls again, and repeatedly, with startling clarity over the water. I'm quite excited, and shovel my double-blades to reach David's boat and ask the question: "What type of whale makes that sound?"

"It's not a whale," David coolly explains. "That's a kelp horn. Someone cut off the bulb of a kelp and is blowing into it. But be patient. The real sounds will come."

About two hours into the trip we disembark for lunch at the Blinkhorn Peninsula. Getting out of the boat, I almost crumple, my legs unsteady, like someone who's just grown them. Under the watchful eye of a regal eagle, we snack on salmon and picnic goodies. A local Kwakiutl Indian ambles across the beach and introduces himself as Tom Sewid, grandson of one of the last great chiefs in the region. The name *Sewid*, he tells us, means "Paddling toward the Feast." Tom regales us with local lore, but then really grabs our attention when he relates that yesterday on this very spot he watched as two parent orcas herded their baby into the shallows just off the beach, and proceeded to teach the youngster how to bathe. It was a remarkable sight, one he had never seen nor heard of, and he felt it augured well for our visit. There is a silent consensus: We're paddling toward a visual feast.

An hour later, however, the marine life is still conspicuously absent, though the aerial life is pretty impressive. We see a marbled murrelet, a pigeon guillemot, a pileated woodpecker, a red-necked phalarope, great blue herons, and loons. But no orcas. The only sea life we see is kelp covered with herring roe, and shore crabs. Up in the evergreens we hear Douglas squirrels chittering.

When we arrive at the cove to be our camp, we see that The Other Pod, which had passed us as we listened to Tom Sewid's tales, has arrived first and taken the more elaborate of the sites. Nonetheless, it is a gorgeous roost, and we gleefully unload for our first evening among the orcas, practically vibrating with anticipation.

Yet we neither see nor hear orcas. The night is cut with diesel engines and foghorns, the sounds of night-netters. We rise early and, after a whole-wheat banana-nut pancake breakfast, we shoehorn into our boats and start across the two-mile-wide strait. This is the most dangerous part of the trip, as the open water currents are willful, tricky, and powerful, and we only have a brief window before the tide changes. So over we go, following the dowel-like arms of David, we a wobbly unit with bad rhythm, faces clenched like listening to a loudspeaker test as we dig hard. Water sloshes onto our decks and puddles in our cockpit aprons. Waves fight wind to an uneasy stand-off. Ninety minutes later we're across, in calm water that glistens like distant paddles flashing. We begin to rotor north along a dark viridian sweep of conifers. When we pull in for lunch, there is so much frilly vegetation it reminds me of a yupscale fern bar.

A couple hours later, when we paddle into a narrow bay on Compton's Island, the tide has filled it like a bottle. We berth our boats at White Beach, littered with sun-bleached clam and oyster shells, thick with the smell of brine. Here we go about pitching camp. The local Kwakiutl Indians had half-completed a roof-shelter just above the beach, and beneath it David sets up the kitchen. He pops Sinead O'Conner into his Walkman, passes out Kokanee Glacier Beer, a B.C. brew, and shares what he heard over the radio that The Other Pod had set up camp near here, but fled when a bear wandered into camp. We chuckle at their misfortune, secretly glad it wasn't us, and certain we are on the better road to destiny. Finally we slip off to bed. But just as we're fading into sleep we hear a sound like pages being turned, a rasp and blow, whooshes of air out in the bay—orcas blowing. They're here; we just can't see them. Maybe they'll still be around in the morning.

But the morning is a blushed calm, the sea smooth as molten lead, no sight of whales, no sounds. They've gone wherever whales go.

It is truly a gorgeous day, the light shafting through the moss-strung forest as though it were an image from a motivational poster. We decide to paddle around the island, and in water flat as a Bible belt, the boats glide like a prayer. We stop at a small beach for a nosh and afterwards hike a bough-roofed trail to the highest point on Compton's Island. From the summit we see a black bear rumbling through the shade stripes of the lower woods. Likely he is the same one that came into the camp of The Other Pod the night before, forcing the group to abandon the island, recross Johnstone Strait, and retreat to the first camp, where no whales had been seen.

Back to our boats, and we continue the circumnavigation, ever on the lookout for the telltale spouts of orcas. On the lee of the island we ease through a narrow throat of water, past a granite wall adorned with Kwakiutl pictographs and several midden-beaches with deep carpets of broken shells whitening the shoreline from centuries of shuckings. Then we assume our most splendid attitudes and dock our schooners at the Farewell Harbour Yacht Club on privately owned Berry Island, and offload for lunch and a look around. Behind the hot tub, in the rec room, there is a stunning poster of three orcas, so close I can almost feel their breath. I read the photo credit at the bottom: David Arcese.

After dinner that night, knowing a bear is on the island, we take special care to make sure all edibles are sealed tightly away in the kayak bulkheads. Then, since we still haven't seen any whales, David plays a tape of orcas singing. They sonar click and echo in a way that matches their submarine shape. I begin to wonder if this might be the closest we get to the five-ton mammals, the world's top ocean predator, here in greater numbers than anywhere, or so the brochure claims.

An hour of orca music leaves me tired and disenchanted, like listening to a sold-out Stones concert on the car radio in the parking lot. With the tape still spooling I slouch to my tent.

After blowing up my air mattress, unfurling my bag, and changing to bed attire, I crawl in and shut my eyes. The sounds of orcas drift into my tent like audible smoke, and I wonder if I'm hearing the real thing, or Memorex. Then I sit up in a panic. I remember I left some Reeses peanut butter cups in my shirt pocket, hanging on the line outside my tent. Could these attract a bear? Should I get up and eat them? It's so snug in the bag, and cold outside. I toss back and forth, and finally decide I'll take my chances. Sleep paws in.

The rusty taste of a restless night brings me to consciousness. I check to see if body parts are intact, then go outside to a thick, white fog, where I examine my shirt pocket. The little crown-shaped cups are still there, untouched, and so I pop them into my mouth and start to strike camp. As we're packing the hulls of our boats, David turns on his two-way marine radio and the sounds of orcas spill forth: chirps, warbles, whistles, eerie shrieks, and long keening notes. A dozen seem to be chatting, trading gossip, telling stories of thwarted tourists. They sound so close. Then David reports we're hearing whales on the other side of Johnstone Strait, back at Camp One. The Other Pod, our unfortunate parallel group chased away by the bear, is in the midst of a super-pod (80 to 100 whales), and David's counterpart has put his walkie-talkie to the speaker of his hydrophone for our benefit. The Other Pod is witnessing literally dozens of whales, breaching, splashing, displaying as though for an imperial audience.

So let's go find them. Skipping breakfast, we clamp down hull lids in a hurry and pull our boats over a row of kelp that lies like a continuous windrow along the uneven line of last night's highest tide. The sea here is first a low, lacy line on the sand, then sharp chopped waves like ploughed furrows, then nothing but pale haze, a lush blending with an uncertain sky. Nonetheless, out we go, fueled with hope. Then the fog drops, becoming so thick it's like barging through glue. We can barely see the bow points of our boats as they bevel through the mist. When finally we reach the edge of the strait, David stops and says we have to wait. A Princess cruise ship, or another loveboat, stuffed with tourists looking for whales on high decks with high-powered scopes, could come driving through in this weather and slice into us like a fisherman into halibut.

We have to be patient. Harbor seals, looking like little old bald-headed ghosts, make fluid plunges around us. The trill of eagles seeps from the sulky sky. My feet are cold in my sandals. After twenty minutes with no change in visibility, we pull up onto a cobblestone beach and cook up a breakfast to fuel our upcoming upper-body workout, then play a game of bum-darts to pass time. David reads tides, waves, currents and winds like Bernstein read music, and so we await his word of when. At last, the fog begins to lift. Back into our boats we slip; out to the edge of the strait we glide. It's still too thick to cross, so we sit and wait, wait and sit, all the while listening for the sounds of orcas. All we get are the muzzy blasts of foghorns.

At last a breeze feathers up, and we can see the tops of trees. The airborne counterpart of the orca, a black and white bald eagle, swoops toward our now-apparent route. Our blades spin like windmills as we speed toward the lifting peaks of Vancouver Island. We are now masters of our crafts, whipping the water like aboriginal warriors. By late afternoon we're back at our first campsite, where The Other Pod had sighted the super-pod just hours before.

Now, all is quiet. David hears a report on his marine radio that eight whales are heading our way from Robson Bight, not far southeast, so after a quick pit stop, we jump back in the kayaks and go looking. A close encounter at last seems close at hand. But after thirty minutes of hard paddle time, David hears from a whale-watching boat that the pod has turned around, headed back to the protected Ecological Reserve, off-limits to boaters. So around we turn as well.

Back at camp, as dinner is being prepared, a young boy rows over from his father's trawler and tells us that yesterday an orca swam up to our campside beach and played around for an hour, rubbing himself on the flat stones and pebbles. It was the most amazing display he had ever seen. I feel the expression on my face congeal.

Whales seem to be everywhere but here. Pamela answers a call to nature, and behind a log discovers a papier-mâché model of an orca, which she brings back and places on the dinner table. Just offshore a salmon flings itself out of the water in an amusing defiance of gravity, but it seems more a mockery of an orca's signature performance. At sunset, a cloud, dark as a plum, curls over the 12,000-foot Silver Thorn Mountain in the Coastal Range, and it looks very much like a whale's back.

After dark, we decide to go for one last attempt. We worm into our kayaks and slither into the darkness. The extraordinary bioluminescence of stirred plankton curls around our blades like broken stars spilled into the sea. Still, the mood is blue, ears cocked for the exhalations of an orca. Alas, we hear only the slurping of each other's paddles. And when our small group finally tries to go to sleep, we can't—because in the camp next door, The Other Pod is celebrating their massive whale sighting with a potlatch, lots and lots of liquor, and songs deep into the long northern night.

The next morning, our last on this odyssey, we sit around in the bleed of early light and feel sorry for ourselves. As I sip coffee from a plastic cup with the picture of a spyhopping orca wrapped around its middle, David closes his eyes and a kind of ruined beauty shudders over his face, like the hide of a marine animal disturbed by limpets. David confesses that in twelve years of kayak trips in this area, he has never not seen orcas during an August paddle. The confession doesn't do much to cheer us up. I think we've hit a wall. The whaling wall.

Then Pamela urgently whispers to me, "Look, look, look," like a mourning dove. Out of a combed-back stand of spruce a blacktail deer delicately emerges. He softly strides onto the beach where we've been sipping morning brews. He picks past a pair of gum boots crooked like dead fish on a sandbar. Somehow other motion seems frozen as he strolls past me, pausing just a few feet from the beached boats. A young Japanese girl from The Other Pod cautiously approaches the deer. Instead of running away, the deer reciprocates and gently walks toward the girl. When they meet, the deer seems to plant a deep kiss on the girl's cheek, and the girl puts her arms around the animal's neck in a hug. They exchange looks and touch one another for a minute or so. And then the deer quietly steps back into a stand of trees with leafy branches that hang like waterfalls, and disappears.

It is a scene beyond the quotidian sphere, a coming-together of man and nature seemingly impossible in real life. For a few magical moments I don't harbor Panglossian yearnings for orcas; don't begrudge unfulfilled promises or brochure copy. I only think about the unpredictability of nature, and how accepting it can open up the mind to surprise and wonder, to what the Kwakiutl Indians call *Sewid,* and the serendipity of life on a sea kayak trip in the Inside Passage.

KALIMANTAN

Kenyan Dyak villagers reenact headhunting ceremonies in regalia of their forefathers. Headhunting for the psychic power of the opponent was abandoned a generation ago.

KALIMANTAN
Dancing with the Dayaks

The Law of the Jungle—which is by far the oldest law in the world—has arranged for almost every kind of accident that may befall the Jungle People, till now its code is as perfect as time and custom can make it.

Rudyard Kipling

"The women take possession of the fresh head and start at once their horrible dance with it. I have seen them myself with heads, dripping with blood, and exhaling an awful stench; with devilish joy they were taken by the dancing women, who in their rage—for they get enraged over it—bit the head and licked it, whilst they were dancing through the house like mad women. Horrible!"

When I read this anonymous 1909 account of headhunting in the *Sarawak Gazette,* I knew I had to go to Borneo. I had spent much of a lifetime searching for the essence of true adventure, seeking places where people behaved in a way that was so wildly different from the civilized world that it would be like landing on another planet. Borneo, I thought, must be such a place. The account was written almost a century ago, but Borneo in today's literature is cited as a timeless place, with an interior so remote, so fierce, that it is as untamed now as it was at the dawn of the age of exploration.

I had dug up the *Sarawak Gazette* after receiving an invitation to visit Borneo from a stranger who lived in that strange land. He was a British expatriate who goes by the adopted Dayak name Taman

Kahang. On a visit to the Apo Kayan area of Borneo, he was invited to travel with a Lepo-Tau hunting party (*Lepo-Tau* loosely translates as the "Sun Kingdom People") on its way to Lebusan, a four-day journey trekking over a watershed and paddling *prahus* (solid tree-trunk dugouts) through the rapids of the upper Boh River in the high interior of the island. Taman Kahang was so impressed with the wilderness and guiding skills of the Lepo-Tau that he contacted me, as the company I cofounded, Mountain Travel-Sobek, has a reputation for opening up new adventure destinations. He invited me to join him on a trek through the Apo Kayan and Boh River regions, the homes of the Lepo-Tau, and after doing a bit of research I eagerly accepted. We scheduled the trip for late May, some six months hence.

The third largest island in the world, Borneo has more landmass than California and Nevada fused, but in a steaming jungle landscape—some 750,000 square kilometers of tangled trees, vines, and creepers. And despite the twin juggernauts of bulldozer and chainsaw, the interior holds one of the last great stands of primary forest on the planet. With some 25,000 species of flowering plants (all of Europe has less than 6,000; Africa, about 13,000), it is floristically the richest rain forest in the world. A remote and forbidding land whose impenetrability has preserved many of its mysteries from the leveling scrutiny of the outside world, Borneo even today conjures up visions of bloodthirsty savages, malarial and leech-infested swamps, and explorers being swallowed up by the land or by the poison-dart-toting natives.

The island is not-so-neatly divided among three nations, the results of the crude cuts of the colonialist penknife. The lower two-thirds of the island is Kalimantan (Isle of Mangoes), claimed by the Dutch in the seventeenth century and now part of Indonesia. The northern third, delineated by a watershed that slices through family and tribal groups, is further cut into the Malaysian states of Sarawak and Sabah, and a Liechtenstein of a country on the north coast is the independent but wildly oil rich sultanate of Brunei. To the north, the Philippines. To the south, Java, Bali, and Lombok.

While Sulawesi (formerly the Celebes) guards Borneo's eastern shore, Sumatra and the Malay Peninsula float off its western flank. It is the heart, if not the dark soul, of the Indonesian archipelago.

The word *Dayak* is a generic term loosely denoting any of the more than two hundred tribal communities occupying the inland regions of Borneo. Some are the original inhabitants of the island. For centuries the Dayaks lived in isolation in lowland regions, but when the Islamic Malays started to arrive on the coasts, the Dayaks moved farther and farther inland, not wanting to become part of a religion that among other things prohibits the eating of their favorite food: pork. Today their numbers scratch the million mark, or so experts estimate, as a true census would be impossible; many Dayaks are still nomadic. Archaeologists have found Dayak remains dating back more than forty thousand years and have determined that in ancient times, the tribes of Borneo ate the same food and wore much the same ceremonial dress as they do today. From today's vantage, however, it seems to many anthropologists that the Dayak society has enjoyed a long, often sunny, sometimes cloudy day but that twilight has fallen, and soon a rich, complex, fantastic culture will be snuffed into darkness.

With photographer Pam Roberson, I arrived at Sepinggan Airport in Balikpapan the last week in May and was met by Taman Kahang. He proudly pointed out two ironwood pillars standing outside the airport VIP lounge, totems celebrating the abolition of headhunting carved by Dayak Kenyah Lepo-Tau under a contract he helped arrange.

Our first experience in Borneo was a traffic jam, the five o'clock rush hour of Balikpapan. It took thirty minutes to get through town, then Taman Kahang drove us 130 kilometers along the Russian-built highway north to Samarinda, past a panorama of bare trunks and branches, looking more like a New England landscape in early winter than the everlasting summer of the tropics. We were trundling through some of the eight million acres of forest incinerated in a 1983 fire that the government didn't acknowledge and had somehow kept out of the world headlines. That was an amazing feat, since the smoke from the three-month-long fire forced the rescheduling of flights at Singapore's airport, across the South China Sea. The relatively un-regulated logging industry had left the forest floor littered with tinder-dry wood chips and refuse, and that combined with a drought allowed a spark to ignite an area larger than Maryland and increase global deforestation for that year by 50 percent.

In Samarinda, Taman Kahang parked us at the Mesra Hotel, an overpriced, decaying property that once catered to the oil crowd. After dinner he took us to his home to meet his family. Taman Kahang has two sons, Stanley, a newborn, and Van, two, who doesn't yet speak—perhaps because he's confused by the many languages spoken to him: Bahasa Indonesia, by his peers; Dayak Kenyah, by his mother; and English, by his father. His wife, Farida, not long back from London, looked as though she'd been properly outfitted at Harrod's. We also met Farida's mother, Len Usat, who was impressively adorned with a full complement of fifty brass rings dangling from her pierced, elongated lobes. Len Usat's ears were perforated when she was thirteen, though, at the time, many girls were started within days of birth. (Piercing is rarer among men.) At first, just wooden pegs are inserted into tiny cuts in the ear lobes, then small rings are attached to the perimeter of the ear. Gradually the number and size of the rings are increased, and the lobe is stretched continuously until it hangs like a lasso. The longer the lobe and the more rings attached, the more beautiful the maiden, at least in the old days. Today, the custom has almost died out in favor of the Western fashion of simple pierced ears, with tiny earrings that seem almost a mockery of the original tradition.

My visit had multiple purposes. I was curious about this mysterious island and its infamous headhunting peoples, and I wanted to see firsthand what its wild jungles might reveal. Taman Kahang had arranged for us to join another group of Lepo-Tau on a journey over land and water to the interior of the island that would include two never-before-seen reenactments of headhunting history that I didn't want to miss. But I was also on a reconnaissance mission to see if there might be an adventure tour to be designed here, one that would lure travelers back to travel in my footsteps and perhaps paddle down a wild river deep in the heart of Borneo. Our itinerary would take us to the village of Long Lebusan, and from there I would work my way deeper and deeper into the darkness.

Long Lebusan lies in a beautiful dell between the razor-toothed mountains of the Menyapa Range to the south and east, and the hanging spurs of the Apo Kayan Plateau to the north and west. *Long* simply means "river confluence," which is where many Dayak villages are situated. Long Lebusan is made up of some 437 residents. That's down some fifty people in a year, lost to the irresistible lures of the lowlands, including lifesaving medicine, doctors, and hospitals.

The riches of Long Lebusan are another problem altogether. The Dayak Kenyah of Lebusan have discovered placer gold in the Boh River. They know it is a blessing, but sense it could be a curse. To date the government has not recognized land sovereignty for the Kenyah, and in fact no highlands Dayak village in East Kalimantan has received a land title. The Dayak Kenyah of Lebusan believe that in the not-too-distant future outsiders, entrepreneurs, carpetbaggers, and foreign companies will be awarded contracts and concessions to mine the gold of the Boh River, and the people of Lebusan will lose out—not just in the monies they feel should be their own but in the rape of their culture, inevitable if a rush for gold began. To stay ahead, the Lepo-Tau would like to find a way to trade their gold before it's too late. It takes too long to trek it to the coast, and Mission Aviation Fellowship (MAF), an alliance of different religious denominations that pool resources to serve the most obscure and dangerous airstrips in the world, mostly with single-engine Cessnas, has no regular service here and frowns on employing their higher-purpose planes for crass commerce.

Taman Kahang tells me he'd like to convince an American white-water rafting team to come to Lebusan with some white-water inflatables to make the first descent of the eighty-kilometer-long Boh River gorge, which begins just downstream from the village. To trek around the gorge can take weeks; but no *prahu* has ever successfully navigated the narrow, twisting canyon that spills the Boh off the plateau, the white-water boating skills of the Kenyah notwithstanding. The rapids in the gorge are just too big for the heavy, unwieldy *prahus*. Below the gorge the Boh flattens out, becomes navigable, then joins the Mahakam, which in turn runs to Samarinda before emptying into the Makassar Strait connecting the Sulawesi and Java Seas. Taman Kahang's idea is to persuade a group of adventurers to undertake this expedition, barging along the best of the Lebusan boatmen as crew, teaching them how to pilot the rafts, then leaving the rafts behind for the Dayaks. They could then use the boats to bring their gold and other goods—such as the aloe wood found in the area—to the coast in a reasonable time frame. To get the rafts back, since they are lightweight and roll up to the size of a large backpack, river taxis could be hired, taking the crews and gear to the bottom of the Boh Gorge, and then the gear could be trekked the final distance up to the plateau. It could cut the trade time 50 percent—and, if MAF would fly the rafts back, even more.

I found it an intriguing, enterprising idea and I warmed to it, telling Taman Kahang I'd like to organize such an expedition and return. Funding, as always, would be a problem, as rafts and air tickets don't come cheap, but I promised to give it a try.

We retired early with hopes of catching a flight to the interior the next day. They remained hopes. The Merpati Airlines flight was cancelled because of weather and no new one would be scheduled for several days, as the following day was the last of Ramadan and the Muslims of Samarinda would then be feasting, not working. "Nasi sudah menjad bubuk," Taman said, which translates to "the rice has already turned to porridge," a Dayak version of "no use crying over spilt milk." We were now late, and if we could not get to the highlands soon the actors in the two plays would return to their rice paddies.

We spent the day trying to line up a flight. The most likely source seemed to be MAF, and they put us on their waiting list.

At noon the following day, we received word from MAF that if we could gather everything together in thirty minutes, they could squeeze in an unscheduled flight, at the unholy rate of $650 total. (The normal rate was $30 per person, and there were four in our group: Pam, Taman, Farida, and me.) It was worth it, we felt, so as not to miss the reenactments, something that increasingly fascinated me, both for a chance to witness a lurid history, but also to see how these proud people were accommodating social and economic change. American Paul Lay, the pilot of the Cessna 185, had easily made a thousand flights under all conditions to the interior, yet he still got excited and pitched the plane into a steep circle as we buzzed over two black hornbills, the fruit-eating birds bigger than eagles prized by the Dayaks for their feathers and ivorylike beaks—and now an endangered species, something I felt we were about to become until Paul pulled out of his spin.

Late in the afternoon we landed at the year-old dirt strip of Long Ampung, on some maps called Muarajalan, just one degree, forty-two minutes north of the equator, a thousand meters high and steam-bath hot. Nobody was there to greet us. We were a day and a half late, and the welcoming party had given up on us. So Taman Kahang trotted the half a mile to the village while we stayed behind with the gear.

In an hour a dozen small boys filed onto the strip, hoisted our heavy kits onto their backs, and marched down the trail, with Pam, Farida, and me in tow. We crossed the Kayan River on a swinging bridge and passed a series of rice storage sheds on stilts (to keep out rats) with metal padlocks on the doors (to keep out the human rats—a sign of the times and of location, being close to the airstrip). Then we passed the three local churches—Protestant, Catholic, and KINGMI, which is an Indonesian acronym for Gospel Tabernacle Christian Church of Indonesia. The missionaries are in keen competition here for a piece of a rich new-flock pie. And finally we came upon the main long house.

Literally a long house, it looks like a narrow warehouse on stilts, built without nails and triangularly roofed like a barn. It sits about fifteen feet off the ground to protect its residents from snakes, wild animals, flooding, and, in the past, headhunting parties, as the only access is by a notched ladderlike log that would be pulled up in the evenings. It also makes for a cooler residence than earthbound shelters. A long verandah, or gallery, runs the length of the 300-meter-long building, a thoroughfare where rice is pounded, mats woven, fishing nets repaired, *rappats* (leaderless, consensus-seeking communal meetings) are held, and ceremonies performed. From the rafters of the porch trophy heads used to be hung like Christmas ornaments, but no longer. The government threatened to torch the long houses unless the collected heads were buried. Off the verandah are doors to separate family apartments, called *lamins,* and inside, the floor planks, cut from giant dipterocarp trees, are covered with woven rattan mats and, in Long Ampung, linoleum strips as well.

Once in the long house we were ushered into a dark back room that turned out to be the chief's apartment. His name is Pemgbung, but Taman Kahang said most visitors call him Ping Pong. A father ten times over who chain-smoked and looked like a less-logical Mr. Spock with his hanging looped ears, he was seventy years old.

We exchanged pleasantries and signed his newly started guest book (we were the second entry, the first in five months). Then we accepted a wad of glutinous boiled rice served wrapped in banana leaves and some sweet whole pineapples. We begged an early retirement, as Pam and I still had a bit of jet lag. But Taman Kahang stayed up most of the night haggling with Ping Pong over the price of porters to carry our gear to Long Uro. When last he was here the price was $1.80 per person for the four-hour trek, but now they wanted $3.00 each. A Swiss tour group taking advantage of the new airstrip had offered the higher price, and now the young porters refused to work for less. And to add fuel to the fire, Ping Pong presented Taman Kahang with a bill for the food we had eaten. In the not-so-old days guests could stop in and expect unbridled hospitality, including meals, but the Swiss group had offered inflated prices for the food presented and that turned heads.

Taman Kahang, who is a sincere advocate of an improved Dayak economy, was disturbed by the precedent of short-sighted greed and pleaded that we were not tourists—our mission was of a higher nature, and they should take that into account. But the Dayaks refused to lower their price. It looked like a standoff. Taman Kahang retired to the back of the Long House for a rest, and we waited. Then later in the afternoon Panyang Alung, Taman Kahang's fifty-year-old father-in-law, walked in from Long Uro and volunteered to help carry the gear. Ping Pong also offered to help, and a couple of the village girls said they would pitch in for the old price. So, with a makeshift army of volunteers, we filed out of Long Ampung, leaving the young men behind with empty pockets but a certain pride intact.

It was a hot hike. The humidity squeezed like the rank coils of an unseen snake, pressing the good air from our lungs. I had a touch of diarrhea, and after I had ducked behind a bush for the third time, Panyang Alung picked some berries he called *siap bahii* and urged me to swallow them. Almost immediately I was sealed up, back on track. We passed a cave painted with intricate, curvilinear designs of birds and spirits. Panyang Alung said the cave was where, in the past, heads were often lopped, and he did a mock demonstration with his *parang* (a home-forged, iron-bladed machete) against Pam's neck. We crossed three precarious bridges before stepping past a partial clearing where the original highlands mission was established in 1932. The American missionaries there had failed to convert the majority of the animist Kenyah at Long Uro, so they moved upriver, cleared a new site, built a new church, and took their few converts with them. That outpost prospered to become Lidung Payau, thirty minutes' walk away, and eventually Christianity spread back and took over Long Uro as well.

As we were about to cross the final suspension bridge spanning the Kayan River, a delegate from Long Uro ran over and implored us to wait. The welcoming procession wasn't yet ready. Minutes later they gave us the cue, and we stepped over the swinging bridge, through a cloud of black smoke from a welcoming fire, and up to a procession line of the entire village. The women were spectacularly outfitted in brilliant gold-and-silver embroidered *kain songkets,* while the men wore ordinary clothes. One had on a polyester tee shirt that said "Bull-Shirt," while a one-legged man dubiously announced on his outer-wear that he was a member of the "Oregon Jogging Club"; such were the articles donated by the missionaries in an effort to evolve the lo-cal habit from the traditional natural-fiber wear from the forest.

Pam and I worked the procession like politicians at a fund-raiser, pumping hands with every village member, even the babies, though neither side of the shaking wrists could communicate beyond bliss-ful grins and vigorous head nods. Once at the end of the line we were led into another long house, this one more Spartan than Long Ampung's, and over pineapple slices and bananas we were introduced to Peding Bid, the grandson of Jalung Apui, who was a central figure in the reenactment of a peace conference we would be viewing here. Peding Bid, who walked with a limp, was an old and ailing man, but he was happy to see us, and happy that there would be a celebration of his famous grandfather.

Glancing around the long house left little doubt as to the aus-terity of Long Uro. Except for two posters, one of Jesus, the other a cheesecake calendar for a Jakarta food company, nothing adorned the walls. The room was uncluttered, containing only an ancient Standard-brand sewing machine, a row of large, dragon-design Ming Dynasty storage vessels called *tempayans,* some brass gongs, a single-shot rifle, and a wood-frame bed hung with a white sheet. There were no tables, no chairs, no furniture of any kind—and this in the middle of an island that has been called the Saudi Arabia of Southeast Asia, the greatest oil depot east of Iran. Brunei, on the north coast, distrib-utes its oil revenue among its people, and it has one of the highest per-capita incomes in the world. The joke goes, when a Brunei citi-zen runs out of gas, he buys a new car. But in Kalimantan, less than eighty kilometers away on the same island, the per-capita income is among the world's leanest. In Kalimantan the oil money flows to Java and to the multinational oil companies. If it stayed within the borders, the Dayaks would be flush. As we sat on the floor and traded curious looks, Taman Kahang pulled out some packages of tomato, carrot, and onion seeds and handed them to our hosts. Although in Dayak there is no word for "thank you," it was clear they were overwhelmed with gratitude. They felt rich.

Long Uro is about a hundred fifty years old, ancient by Dayak Kenyah standards. Few villages make it to the century mark. The reason: swidden agriculture, which is the slash-and-burn, or shifting-cultivation, technique. The soil is poor in Borneo, and the nutrients are quickly leached out, leaving the ground fallow after a few plantings. The life-supporting fields worked by each village are pushed farther back into the jungle every few years, until eventually there is no arable land within a reasonable walking distance and the entire village must move. In Long Uro, the nearest paddies are ninety minutes' walk away. Thirty years ago the fields here were much closer, but the elders knew they were running out of time, so several families packed up and moved south to the fecund banks of the Boh River and started the offshoot village of Long Lebusan.

After a dinner of venison from a freshly killed mouse deer, it was announced there would be an evening of celebratory dancing on the long-house gallery. This is the common form of entertainment among Dayaks, like going to the opera, a concert, or the movies for much of the Western world. At the appointed hour the entire village gathered on the floor of the verandah. From the rafters hung a *keluri*, a dried gourd shaped like a chemical retort with a hundred cigarettes projecting in a bundle from its bulb. These were peace smokes, which would be toked by the tribal chiefs in the re-created peace conference later. Two men sat near the front of the crowd and began to play high-pitched, rattan-stringed, lutelike instruments called *sambas,* in a tune that sounded like "Dueling Banjos." A group of dancers emerged from one of the apartments and performed an elegant sun dance called *Nari Preng,* swaying their bodies like rice blowing in the wind.

Two men, adorned in traditional battle gear, next performed

Kancet Pepatai, a pas-de-deux warrior dance that in earlier times was performed before a headhunting expedition. The men wore war helmets, woven rattan caps set with black, yellow, and crimson beads and topped with six long black and white plumes from the tail of the helmeted hornbill. War coats made from the skin of the largest cat in Borneo, the clouded leopard, were worn like jerkins, with taken "heads" placed through openings in the front of the skin. Armbands and leglets of rattan cords pinched their skin. Around their waists, slung on rattan belts and sheathed in silver scabbards, were *parangs* to outshine all other *parangs,* with hilts intricately carved in horn from the antlers of the *kijang,* the Borneo barking deer. In their left hands they held elongated, diamond-shaped, cork-wood shields, from the center of which huge masks regarded us implacably, their eyes red, their teeth the painted tusks of wild boars. Thick black tufts of hair hung in neat lines down either edge and across the top and bottom of the shields, tufts of hair that, in another time, would have been taken from the scalps of heads cut off in battle.

The dance began with a bow to the audience. Then the men bent and turned slowly to the rhythm, wheeling like predators, then facing each other like coiled snakes. The tinkling music grew urgent and was suddenly pierced with savage screams. The men took long strides toward one another, stomping their feet with great force. Then, with whiplike movements, they leapt violently, weaving, dodging, lunging, and striking as though cutting heads like corn. Then all at once it was over, and the crowd cheered and clapped. I wasn't sure whether to give a standing ovation for the sheer theater of it all, or to politely clap for a piece of fakery that in some ways devalued their own heritage. I took the middle ground and clapped with the best of them.

Next, the women danced the *Enggang* feather dance, one that simulates the flight of the hornbill, the enggang bird, the Kenyah symbol of peace and unity. The dance was simple yet expressive, dignified but provocative, a delicate poem of subtle arm movements, genteel turns, and graceful swoops, a ballet full of politeness. It was deliciously fragile after the violence of the men. With small, flowing movements of their wrists and fingers, all in synchrony, their arms rippling, their supple bodies undulating slightly, it was a refined and elevated art, coming from one of the most remote villages on the planet. It made me think of a scene from the Roland Joffe film, *The Mission,* in which an eighteenth-century Jesuit father is trying to convince a papal emissary that the South American Guarani Indians are more than savage heathens and deserve to have their mission preserved. He arranges for a group of naked boys to perform a lyric cantata chorus, with a soprano that is so clean, so celestially beautiful, that it would appear no further argument as to the eminent humanity of these people need ever be proffered.

But those in power are not always persuaded by talent and art, especially when it is displayed in an incongruous milieu. Before the trip I was rummaging through the library and found an out-of-print book called *A Stroll Through Borneo,* by James Barclay. In the book, Barclay had dug up a letter written by a missionary in 1930 who had witnessed the same Dayak dance I had just seen so beautifully performed: "This dance is something that will be cast off very quickly once the light of the Gospel penetrates the Dayak heart . . . the rhythm and grace of these dances is undeniable, and yet they too will vanish with other heathen customs when the Lord Jesus comes into their lives." Thank God, to date, though Christianity has come to the Dayaks, the dances survive.

To bring a climax to the evening's show, one of the dancers, a fine-featured, aristocratic-looking lady, approached Pam, took her hand, and led her back into the *lamin.* Minutes later Pam emerged fully dressed in the spangled Kenyah costume, with a tuft of hornbill feathers attached to each hand, fixed like open fans. The *sambe* players immediately struck up a lilting tune. The corner of Pam's mouth twitched in nervousness as she bowed to the audience from the proscenium, but the music was hypnotic and she was soon swept up in her own dance, mesmerizing the crowd as well. She danced with tremulous majesty, a slow, yearning, graceful dance, the long fan feathers sweeping over her body in alternating curves. When she finished, the whole village broke into an ascending chant of appreciation, called *Le-Maluck*, which is similar to a standing ovation given when a performer does something extra special. Peding Bid, the grandson of Jalung Apui, hung a tightly beaded necklace with a pendant of two metallic, imitation pig's tusks around her neck. Then the aristocratic, high-cheekboned woman, with the dignified air of the Queen Mother bestowing a knighthood, stepped to Pam and pressed another necklace of appreciation into her palm. With her personal interpretation of their art, Pam had touched the Dayaks of Long Uro.

I was then asked to follow in Pam's dance steps and was conned into battle gear, complete with *kliaus* (the battle shield) and *parang* (the sine qua non sword), and asked to dance to the same tune. I could never compete with Pam's degree of elegance, so I did my Michael Jackson imitation (he needn't worry) and then pulled out a couple of sparklers I had purchased on an impulse from a Chinese merchant in Samarinda. I lit the sparklers and did my version of a flash dance, which frightened and wowed the big-eyed audience, who had never seen such a sight and seemed a bit worried I might light their long house on fire. But as the sparklers fizzled to their last spark, the appreciative crowd broke into applause and hummed their ultimate tribute, the haunting *Le-Maluck* drone-chant.

As is customary for visitors, we slept on the long house floor, in a mosquito-netting tent that we had brought with us from the United States and called our "short house." We drifted off to a chorus of cicadas ringing like some carillon of tiny but insistent bells, and were awakened at dawn by a tremendous cacophony of roosters crowing, geckoes chick-chacking, babies crying, women pounding rice in the large porch mortises, and children running across the noisy floor planks. It's nearly impossible to tiptoe across a long house floor, and that is by design; the planks traditionally were laid loosely so headhunting parties couldn't sneak up on a sleeping family. There are no more surreptitious headhunting visitations, but the clattering floor boards persist today, one Dayak custom that unfortunately doesn't seem to be threatened.

The first order of a Dayak day is the taking of a bath and a bowel movement, both done in the river. (Drinking water is collected upstream.) The men go naked to bathe, but are careful to conceal their genitals with cupped hands. The young women are modest and keep their sarongs tied under the armpits as they bathe, but the old ones sit contentedly in the shallows, naked from the waist up, leathery and withered, hair screwed up in graying knots. As we trotted down to do our duties, we passed a conventional-looking outhouse off the path sitting in a mud pool, looking unused and out of place. Taman Kahang, with his vision to help turn Long Uro into a tourist attraction, had flown it up unassembled from the coast, and in his absence the Lepo-Tau had put it together, but had placed it over the wrong medium. Its off-the-beaten-track site notwithstanding, there had been no tourists to employ the facility, and the villagers certainly preferred the alfresco circumstance of the river.

After a breakfast of pea soup and bamboo shoots mixed with rice, we were led to a path outside Long Uro, where the Lepo-Tau reenacted, for the first time since the real thing, a headhunting raid. What they didn't show was the preparation that used to go into such a raid. Before going into battle, the Dayak Kenyah warriors were not allowed to have sexual intercourse for at least a week; they slept together in a special room apart from their women; and during the day they trained outside the village so they would not even see a female. Even their food, which was cut back to half-rations with just one cup of water a day for a minimum of seven days, was served to them by boys. On the actual day of battle they were not allowed to eat or drink anything. In James Barclay's book, he says it was believed the Spartan practices would sharpen their awareness and increase their discipline during the actual attack.

In the play we witnessed, a group of Ibans, a rival Dayak tribe, was walking down the forest path to their fields and paused for a lunch break. Then from out of the bush on all sides the Kenyah Lepo-Tau ambushed the Ibans. Some of the attackers wore genuine battle gear, passed down from grandparents, consisting of vests fashioned from sun-bear pelts, hats with war feathers, and mother-of-pearl breastplates. Others, less fortunate in their inheritances, wore cardboard vests painted with feathers, kitchen colanders as breastplates, and Western-style shorts and tee shirts, one announcing the warrior was a "break-dancer." *Parangs* flashed, arms flailed, throats screamed, and bodies fell. There was much parrying, feinting, and dodging, and one Iban escaped in flight. It was all too real, with blood lust clearly etching the faces of the Lepo-Tau and fear coursing through the Ibans. After the last of the Ibans was struck down, the victims, who collapsed with their backs toward us, buried their heads in their chests, so that from our vantage it truly looked as though they had been decapitated.

When the dust of battle cleared, the Lepo-Tau picked up the bodies and started to carry them back toward the village. "Cut!" the director seemed to yell, a village elder watching the show from the sidelines. "It's all wrong. Take two." It appeared the Lepo-Tau had committed a grievous script error when they started to cart the bodies away, something that was never done in real headhunting raids. So they started from the top and ran through the entire scene again, but this time, once the Ibans were dead the Lepo-Tau pretended to bury them in shallow graves in the brush adjacent to the path. It was a take. Cut and wrap. I felt as though I were watching a Cecil B. DeMille epic in the making rather than any genuine ceremony.

We next followed the victorious warriors as they paraded home after a long day of hunting heads. As they climbed up onto the long house porch, the women lined up, dressed in their finest, and congratulated their men folk with gong banging and singing. Then the men broke into games of celebration, including one in which rounded rocks and a huge gourd, head facsimiles, were bowled back and fourth down the gallery planks amongst a riotous chorus.

It was time for a respite. We sat down to a long prayer, one that precedes every Christianized Dayak meal, then supped on shredded wild boar with rice, capped with bites of the posterior of an insect so big that anywhere else it would have required a pilot's license. After a brief siesta, the villagers wanted to continue with their celebration of the headhunting era. With wads of clay for rocks, they demonstrated how young boys were trained to prepare for a headhunting expedition. The 1909 account in the *Sarawak Gazette* also declaimed how the young were prepped for the rigors of headhunting:

"Justly are the Dayaks called head-hunters, for during the whole of their life, from early youth till their death, all their thoughts are fixed on the hunting of heads. It is the first thing for the Dayak grandmother to teach her grandchildren—it is the last thought of the dying Dayak. The child, unable to speak, scarcely able to walk, is addressed by his grandmother in the following way: "Listen well, my rice, my rice-basket, we put all our confidence in you, for you have to avenge us. For the head of your grandfather or some other member of your family is hanging somewhere over the fireplace, and you have to avenge us. Let us not confide in you in vain, let it not be in vain that we educate you and carry you to the river to bathe; let us not have given you our milk in vain."

Fresh heads were integral to good harvests, but other now-defunct rituals were equally important, and the Lepo-Tau tried to bring them back. They performed a stick dance, wherein they pounded planting poles on the floor, symbolically striking the birds and diseases that might otherwise destroy a crop. And they planted bamboo stalks flayed at the top, where raw eggs were placed, offerings to the Kenyah goddess Bungan Malan, who has a fondness for chicken embryos.

At last it was time for the main acts: the life and times of Jalung Apui, who was recognized as the first and only king of all the Kenyah peoples, followed by a reenactment of the peace conference. In reality there were two conferences, about twenty years apart. The reenactment of the first conference would take place later, at Long Lebusan. For reasons beyond me, we would be witnessing the second conference reenactment first—perhaps because memories were stronger of the latter, and Long Uro had first pick.

Before the review could begin the village knelt in prayer, asking God's permission to bring back their unholy time for the benefit of their visitors. Then it began in earnest, with a procession of women slowly shuffling to the beat of a gong down the verandah of the long house, carrying a continuous length of chain at their sides. The chain symbolized their unity and linkage in the Peace Conference. I couldn't help but notice that the women, even the young ones, had the traditional looped earlobes hanging on their shoulders, and it wasn't until I looked closely that I could see these weren't flesh at all—rather, flesh-colored strands of rattan doing an excellent impression of ears from that era. My goodness, I thought, even their ears aren't real. Marching around a huge effigy of the enggang bird, the symbol of peace, the women wrapped the chain around a Chinese jar and covered it with a gong. Inside the jar were the souls of all the Kenyah peoples, and the gong placed on top was a lid of protection.

Jalung Apui had persuaded the leaders of the eighteen neighboring subtribes to attend this peace conference, a miraculous achievement, considering the times. Dayak Kenyah oral history tells that, in conjunction with his efforts at the peace conference, Jalung Apui visited "Tuan Rajah," the White King of Sarawak—Charles Brooke (son of Sir James)—at his palace in Kuching, on the Sarawak coast. They agreed to work together to eliminate headhunting, and Brooke sealed their accord with several gifts, a few of which were on display in Long Uru, such as Sumatran tiger skin, a tarnished bronze Victorian fruit bowl, and two *maniks,* precious lacquered glass beads believed to have been traded from Venice, via China, in Marco Polo's time.

In November 1924, a little more than a decade after Jalung Apui's second peace conference, Vyner Brooke, Charles's son, held what he called "The Great Peace Council" in the village of Kapit, on the Rajang River in central Sarawak. It was attended by a Dutch civil and military delegation, British envoys, and hundreds of Dayak tribal chiefs. It was heralded worldwide as the conference that ended headhunting in Borneo, and Western history records Rajah Brooke as the humanitarian hero who orchestrated the watershed event. In the articles of the time, and in subsequent books and accounts, there is no mention of Jalung Apui, the Tensing Norgay to Brooke's Hillary, a local hero who quietly stood in the shadows but whom many say deserve the lion's share of credit.

Of course, headhunting didn't just disappear after Brooke's Kapit conference. As a practice it ebbed in the 1940s, then dribbled into the 1950s. Ironically, last heads taken may have been by the British, when troops were sent into the interior to defend Malaysia from Indonesia during the 1963 Confrontation. Incited by the fierce reputation of the Dayaks, the soldiers made a preemptive strike and took four Kalimantan Dayak heads. The story goes that the soldiers brought the heads back to headquarters in Kuching, and the commanding officer was so incensed that he ordered the soldiers back into the jungle to sew the heads back on, so the victims could rest whole in peace.

After the ceremonies, all the players changed to normal attire and squatted around the porch critiquing performances. I, not being able to follow, pulled out Redmond O'Hanalon's classic, *Into the Heart of Borneo*, a book about a spurious quest for the Borneo rhinoceros, which hadn't been sighted in decades, and read a passage that in turn had been pulled from Volume 196 of *The Sarawak Museum Journal*, describing a peculiar Dayak custom called *palang:*

"One of the exhibits that excites the most interest in our museum is that of the palang. This is the tube or rod of bamboo, bone, hardwood, etc. with which the end of the penis is pierced among many inland people. In each end of this center-piece may be attached knobs, points or even blades of suitable material. Some men have two palangs, at right angles through the penis tip.

"The function of this device is, superficially, to add to the sexual pleasure of the women by stimulating and extending the inner walls of the vagina. It is, in this, in my experience decidedly successful.

"We also have a 'natural' palang, exhibited alongside. This is the penis of a Borneo rhinoceros. In the natural state this powerful piece of anatomy has, about four inches behind the tip, a similar sort of cross-bar, projecting nearly two inches out on each side. When tense, this becomes a fairly rigid bar, much like the human palang in general implication. As such, these things were included among the esoterica of inland Long-Houses, along with sacred stones, beads, strange teeth and other charms mainly in connection with human head and fertility ceremonies.

"Many who have handled this pachyderm device have been unable to credit that it is 'genuine.' However, in the untouched state it can be even more impressive. The penis of another male in our possession measures over a foot and a half (relaxed), has a longer tip and cross-piece than the Museum's displayed one."

I had seen this rhinoceros *palang* some months earlier in the Kuching Museum, and now, reading this passage, my curiosity was naturally roused. I looked up at the crowd of men in animated discussion and asked through Taman Kahang if any had a *palang*. To my complete surprise, the assistant chief of Long Lebusan, Pelenjau Serang, who had trekked for five days to witness the celebration, looked at me and nodded.

I was astonished. This seemed the sort of fantastic, apocryphal custom that would filter out of the jungle and be embellished to large type, like the "discovery" of Michael Rockefeller's ingester in New Guinea. And, if the practice had existed, it seemed to me that it would have been one of the first to go under missionary dominion, like the annual let-off-steam, drunken, wife-swapping orgies the Dayaks used to organize, now history. Yet Pelenjau looked at me innocently and asked if I wanted to see his *palang*. I hesitantly replied yes, and, when no women were looking, he indicated I should follow him to the schoolhouse.

Once inside the schoolhouse, Pelenjau locked the door and checked the cracks in the wall to make sure nobody was peeking. He was clearly nervous, and before the unveiling he explained that he was among the last to undergo the operation, that the church and state had indeed persuaded the Dayaks to discontinue the custom, with the promise of a five-year prison term for disobedience. Then he pulled up one side of his shorts and displayed what looked to be the results of an extremely painful operation. Near the tip of his uncircumcised penis a three-inch-long dowel of rattan pierced the flesh. Various materials were used for *palangs*—deer horn, wood, pig bristle, gold, silver, copper wire, and in modern times the shear pins from outboard motors were favored. The accoutrement is supposed to bring great pleasure to women, a sort of troglodytic French tickler, and for the men it was a private statement of bravery. It is never displayed in public and is one of the reasons men cup their privates when bathing.

If a wife tells of her husband's *palang*, it is grounds for divorce, though in the old days no woman of any esteem would condescend to marry a man who was not properly decorated. The crossbar was usually inserted postpuberty, often just before marriage. If the intended was a virgin, the first bar would be the length of the thumb from the middle knuckle to the end of the thumbnail. Then, after a time, a larger one would be inserted, one the length of the little finger from knuckle to nail. And finally, for the ultimate satisfaction, usually after the wife had borne a child or two, a crossbar measuring knuckle to nail on the ring finger would be inset.

For the first time I thought I was witnessing something real in the Dayak culture, a true link to the past, something not created for show but rather something that survived and was hidden away to secure its continued existence.

The operation itself, performed riverside, could be self-executed by driving a six-inch-long sharpened bamboo spike through the flesh just below the glans of the flaccid penis as it was clamped into an instrument shaped like a small bow. There could only be one try. If one couldn't face the self-infliction, he could hire an expert do the deed for about $35. It didn't seem to affect fertility—Pelenjau had six children—but it very often festered into a serious infection, and many Dayaks died postoperatively of septicemia.

It was finally time to leave Long Uro. The men had to get back to the fields; the women had rice to pound. We packed up our dunnage and climbed to the long house porch for goodbyes. There were hardy handshakes, wide grins, and a hundred dollars passed to the *kepala kampung* as a gesture of gratitude for the performances. The noble-looking woman who had given Pam the necklace after her dance a few nights previous, and who looked to be about her age, took Pam's arm and brushed her nose against the back of Pam's hand in a gentle gesture. Then her dark eyes began to tear and cry.

We then headed to Long Lebusan, Long Uro's splinter village, where a reenactment of the first peace conference was scheduled. The route was an old headhunting trail and would take us up the Kayan River close to its source, then southeast, up a pass over a watershed divide and down into the Boh River basin.

Not a mile into the journey, we stopped at a *kubu*, a resting lean-to, and bowed in a long group prayer, asking for a safe trip. Then we trudged into the afternoon heat, bent like beasts of burden, until late in the day we stumbled into the village of Long Sungai Barang, the uppermost Dayak Kenyah village on the Kayan River, with a population of around four hundred people. Closer to civilization than Long Uro, Sungai Barang is a bit richer, with a per-capita income of about sixty dollars a year; and it is a bit looser, with stashes of *tuak* (rice wine), a couple of bottles of which were pulled out to celebrate our visit. It was also a bit cooler, this being one of the highest villages in Borneo, somewhere up around 1,400 meters.

The next morning, as the heavy mist from the Kayan was still rising, giving Sungai Barang a primeval, dawn-of-mankind look, we took to the trail. This would be the longest trekking day. We continued up the Kayan for a time, then turned south and followed a hint of a jungle trail up a pass. The rain forest closed in on us with an airless gloom as we thrashed through a creepered world of endless twi-

light, slogged through mud troughs, and bounced over rank, spring-
ing vegetation, all part of the oldest, richest, most stable ecosystem
on earth. The heat was insufferable, an all-enclosing clamminess that
radiated from the damp leaves, the slippery humus, the great boles of
oaks and chestnuts.

At the first stop I pulled up my pants leg and found a fat leech,
his unctuous head buried in my calf, drunk and happy with the drink
of my blood. I hadn't felt the sucker because the bite of *Haemad-
ipsa zeylanica,* the common ground leech, is painless, containing an
anesthetic in its saliva as well as an anticoagulant. Nonetheless, it
was no fine time watching the turd-brown, rubbery, three-centimeter
worm suck my blood, becoming globular and wobbly in the process. I tried to pull it off me, but his head was anchored deep and
he successfully resisted my efforts. I had heard of all sorts of leech
removal techniques—salt, burning, alcohol, drowning, amputa-
tion—but before I could make an attempt, Pelenjau was hovering
over me with his *parang,* and he shaved the blood-sucker right off,
leaving the head within. Then he pulled out a wad of tobacco from
his pouch, mixed it with spittle, and rubbed the concoction all over
the exposed skin of my legs and feet, the Dayak leech-protection
formula. For double protection he tied tight strings of rattan around
my upper calves, little Berlin Walls for the red-baiters. That was the
holistic part. For post-attack, he quickly carved an exact replica of
a buck knife from a bamboo stalk and stuck it in my belt. I was
ready for the lousy parasites.

For hours we walked through an enchanted forest, any one ten-
hectare plot of which hosted as many as eight hundred different kinds
of trees. Most trees were linked to neighbors by fairy chains of pen-
dulous, festooned lianas, making it seem as though we had stumbled
into some well-decorated hall ready for a celebration. Sometime midday we crested the pass, marked by the call of a gibbon on a high
branch whose gray, furry back was cast with a lattice of sunlight. The
going got easier as we dropped into the streambed of the Muse River,
with delicate hanging plants and vines looking as though they'd been

professionally arranged, alternating between lovely little cascading jewels of tributary waterfalls.

We slogged along, stopping every now and then for a suck on an orange and a leech check (the tobacco juice washed off in the first creek crossing). Pam had set out on the trek wearing long, thin cotton harem pants, but by afternoon they had been shredded to shorts by the forest thorns. Puluck, who was a fit sixty-seven, always stayed out front, trail blazing in his calloused, spatulated bare feet, and once turned around and whacked off the head of a sleek, green coral snake, just before Pam stepped on it. Borneo has the richest snake fauna of Southeast Asia, with some 166 known species, though only 8, such as the coral Pam almost got to know, are deadly poisonous. This snake, I was later told, was the same kind responsible for the condition of the man in Long Uro with the "Oregon Jogging Club" shirt, the man with one leg.

Near twilight, after seven-and-a-half hours of hard trekking, we passed from the somber bluish-greens of the primary forest to the yellowish-olive hues of an expanse of secondary forest, the dregs of now-fallow swidden rice paddies, and walked down to the confluence of the Muse and Dumu Rivers. Another *kubu* provided shelter. It was the only remains of a once-prosperous village, Dumu, which had been abandoned five years ago, now reclaimed by the forest. This was also the farthest point *prahus* could be brought upriver, and two from Pelenjau's voyage from Lebusan ten days previous had been pulled up next to the *kubu*. The area was also buzzing with a blizzard of sweat bees, obnoxious critters that suck body sweat and sting if irritated. So we all fled for the river, stripped, and soaped up, leaving a pile of sweat-soaked clothing on the bank to feed the frenzy. Once washed we had to move slowly and deliberately so as not to perspire, as the smallest bead brought the hordes. Perhaps, I thought, this was the real reason the people of Dumu left.

That night, safely tucked under the mosquito net, downwind from the campfire smoke, Puluck slipped a viscous wad of unidentifiable mush into my hand and indicated I should eat it. I did—it tasted fine, something like spinach—and so he passed me another wad. This time I pulled out my flashlight and examined the snack—sweat-bee embryos. Puluck had somehow raided a sweat-bee nursery and grabbed what he considered a delicacy, and what I now could not.

Before departure downstream the following morning, Pelenjau recited the obligatory prayer for safe passage. Then we piled into the two ten-meter *prahus,* each hewn from a single tree trunk, and started poling downstream. Three Dayaks stood in the bow of each boat and two stood in the stern. In the middle, Pam and I sat on duckboards sandwiched between the duffle on one craft, while Taman Kahang and Farida took midship on the other. As feeder streams found ours the water depth increased, and within an hour our guides took seated positions and traded their poles for paddles.

We glided along through a dark, narrow canyon as though passing through paradise. William O. Krohn, in his 1927 book *In Borneo Jungles,* described a similar voyage: "There is no more beautiful sight than a Dayak boatman . . . always combining perfect poetry of motion with greatest physical efficiency." And I had to agree. I was participating in something that had not changed with the decades. It was cool, pleasant, and effortless, and the scenery was stunning. From the upper branches of a crocodile-tooth tree, a rhinoceros hornbill rustled then wheeled off downstream, as though showing us the way. We ran the moderate-sized rapids, but some were just too steep, requiring portages. These were executed quickly, deftly, as ours was a route traveled many times, dating back at least a century when the Apo Kayan Kenyah would paddle these waters on headhunting expeditions.

At one point, while cruising down the river, there was a sudden lurch of the *prahu* and a stir of commotion as the boatswain frantically pointed to a black blur on shore, and the rest of the crew shifted paddles into high gear. Craning to get a better look, I watched the blur slip into the water and slither toward us at an astonishing speed.

"It's a king cobra," Taman Kahang yelled to me from the other boat, which was several lengths ahead. Fine, I thought. The king cobra, or *hamadryad,* is the largest venomous snake in the world—

up to six meters long—and has a reputation for aggressiveness. Pelenjau had lost three dogs to a king cobra the month before. James Barclay described an incident on a similar downriver excursion in which a king cobra swam out to his boat then crawled on board. He was barely able to knock it away with his umbrella. We didn't have umbrellas, but one of our guides pulled out a single-shot rifle and readied his aim. We were quicker than the snake, however, and sailed around the corner before there was damage from either side.

With the rifle ready, though, the crew decided to drift down the side of the bank to look for *babi*, wild boar, a Dayak delicacy. Almost immediately one appeared to emanate from the thick green leaf matting and at once disappear back into it like flowing mud. No meat for lunch, it seemed, but we paddled up a tributary, tossed weighted conical nets called *jala* into the currents, and pulled out a big flat fish resembling a sole. We wouldn't go hungry.

Our little river merged with the larger Boh, and the *prahus* were moored with their rattan painters to a buttressed tree. Up the bank was a food cache of bamboo tubes crammed with boiled rice and the rank, sun-baked jerky from a bearded pig that had been speared on the upriver journey ten days ago. A fire was started, the fish was roasted, and we sat down to a respectable meal in the middle of the Borneo rain forest. Over bites of the putrid-smelling *babi*, one of the guides told us that his father had been killed by Ibans in a headhunting raid near here some years ago. He remembered the retaliatory expedition launched against the Ibans, one in which after nine days of tracking, six were caught and decapitated, and as the trackers had no food, they ate two of the victims. Our storyteller told us he remembered the men from his village returning after the avenging hunt with the taken heads, and that he and the other village boys, in their Rousseauean innocence, were kept amused playing with the skulls for weeks around the long house.

That night we pitched camp on a broad beach on the western bank of the Boh, less than a mile upstream from Ternak, the most dangerous cataract of our journey. Huge dark clouds were pilling up across the rivers, so the guides unsheathed their *parangs* and set to work building waterproof lean-tos out of bamboo and wide, succulent leaves. It poured hard all night, dropping a significant percentage of the five meters of rain the area receives a year, but we all stayed dry.

The next morning, Pam's birthday, a saffron butterfly floated onto her toothbrush, then fluttered off downstream toward the great rapid. We arrived an hour later at its entrance, a gray-walled gorge that took a sharp turn so the guts of the cascade couldn't be seen, though the ominous noise of arguing currents ahead could be heard. Pelenjau and crew unloaded some of the more precious gear and took off on a thirty-minute portage around the kilometer-long rapid. Pam and Farida followed, deciding not to risk running the rapid in the tipsy *prahus,* one of which had capsized and almost been lost on the earlier, upstream journey.

With a blue grip on the gunwales, I answered, "I'm ready, I think," to Pelenjau as he shoved us into the swirls, and we were swept toward Ternak. It was a violent descent. Through the thunder of incoming water I could hear the frantic, staccato commands of Pelenjau, who was ruddering the rear. Through the curls of spray, rocks reared up and shot past us as the boatmen feverishly struggled to keep a purchase on the current. There were three distinct falls in Ternak, and at each one it seemed as if the canoe were about to spear itself into a rock when, at the last instant, a coordinated flash of paddles would swerve us into the rebounding water. The craft rolled left and right, bobbed up and down as we hurtled through the white, churning water, until suddenly we had all purled into an eddy, where Pam and Farida were waiting, plucking leeches from their jungle portage.

An hour downstream we passed fields of beans and maize, the good works of the village of Long Lebusan. At the insistence of Pelenjau, we pulled over to the bank, tied up the boat, and walked through a sugarcane field to survey the prospects of a partially razed patch of level ground—a new airstrip was being cleared, with hopes of attracting larger and more frequent aircraft than does the current mudway that serves as an airstrip for the occasional mission flights that land here.

A few more paddle strokes downriver, and we met the Lebusan River, clear and shallow. It was raining, a good sign for arriving guests, said Penlenjau. Paddles were stowed, the poles once again pulled out, and our crew powered the *prahus* up some riffles and parked in the waterfront lot of Long Lebusan.

It had been almost two weeks since our ten-member team had seen their friends and relatives in Long Lebusan, but it was not a happy reunion. The first news was that a fever had been going around, and just yesterday two baby girls had died. Most of the villagers were wearing pink headbands in mourning, and an exuberant, arabesque-designed structure was festooned with red, yellow, and white cloth— a mausoleum for the deceased children.

Despite the pall of grief, the people, upon seeing our arrival, quickly slipped into their ceremonial clothing and lined up for a welcoming procession. They draped colorful leis around our necks, flashed gold-toothed smiles, and told us we were the first non-missionary Americans to ever visit their village.

After the welcoming procession, Baya Udau, the chief of group ceremony and *adat* for Long Lebusan, led us to a three-room structure across from the soccer field and said it would be ours for the duration of our visit. It had been the house of a Muslim, of the Bugi tribe, a trader who had privately flown in cooking pots, steel tools, the coveted salt and other items, and set up shop to trade for gold. He made his fortune and left. Baya Udau gave us a padlock and key and offered to have a guard watch the place while we were out. This seemed odd, in a small, remote village in which crime of any nature would be difficult to achieve and more so to conceal. Taman Kahang took me aside and explained that one of the young Lepo-Tau who had emigrated to the lowlands had become a renowned professional thief, and he was presently back in Long Lebusan visiting relatives. Taman Kahang himself had been ripped off in lowland Tanjung Manis by the thief, who was especially clever with his craft. We were obvious targets and had to take extra precautions. In Taman Kahang's view, the thief was a casualty of civilization. In the recent past, when the *adat* of the Kenyah was the highest principium and rubric of village life, such behavior would have been unthinkable. But the codes of the coast, including material success at all costs, were encroaching.

After we settled in, crushing a dozen giant spiders on the walls of our little house as we did so, we bolted the windows from the inside, locked the door, and stepped out to the soccer field, where the villagers were preparing their reenactments. In Long Uro we had witnessed the second great peace conference organized by Jalung Apui; now we would see the first one, and several related events of that era that have survived to the present. It all began with a tug of war. In Jalung Apui's years, when it was near harvest time, all the villagers would gather in an open field and stretch a rattan rope with the men on one end, women on the other. With a signal, both sides would pull, and if the men won, it meant a good yield; if the women overpowered, it meant bad crops. The whole setup seemed to guarantee the correct outcome, the natural size differences of the sexes even more so, but we watched the contest, cheering like basketball fans as the rope went taut, twenty-five men on one side, eighteen women on the other. Then it snapped, sending both sides collapsing back into human piles.

"What does that mean? I asked Pelenjau, who was judging the match.

"It means there will be no disease on the crops," he snapped back, as fast as the rope.

Next we witnessed a series of demonstrations: how the Dayak Kenyah make a two-and-a-half-meter blow pipe, still used today; how they boil the sap from the *upas* tree, turning it to a potent strychnine-like poison, and cook it on darts. They displayed fourteen different herbs and plants gathered from the surrounding forest and told us how they were used for infections, swellings, itching, backaches, muscle cramps, coughs, exhaustion, congestion, and other ailments. They demonstrated the Dayak deep-tissue massage; basket making;

and the setting of animal traps, placed around the paddies to keep rodents and civet cats away. They showed how they inspected the nipple positions of newborn dogs; wrong arrangement and the pup would have to be drowned. They took us to Pelenjau's eighty-nine-year-old mother, Iring Alung, who was the last in their village to have traditional indigo tattoos decorating her legs. A series of concentric rings meant to be a part-snake, part-bird, and part-plant design, they identified her tribe, family, and station. She had it done when she was a young bride, the pattern punctured into her skin with brass needles hammered with a stick, the ink a mixture of tree sap and black ash from cooking pots. It was a torturous process and once completed, it was three months before she could walk again. The Kenyah men of the past would tattoo their hands, one imprint for every head taken. The church had put an end to tattooing, but Iring Alung was still proud of her markings, flattered we wanted to see them.

That evening, while the wet air was filled with the sounds of vi-brating membranes of thousands of cicadas, we were visited by Pekuleh Bilung, the seventy-year-old shaman who was the chief of tribal group ceremony and *adat* for the whole of the Boh region. He was also a wizard of much repute and once performed his good magic for Sukarno, or so he said. Such sorcerers were once among the most powerful and esteemed personages in the Dayak cosmology. They had to be consulted for every major village decision and were sought after for healing magic, fertility blessings, and general advice. The mission-aries stripped the shamans of their potency, telling the villagers that to practice magic was unholy and would not be tolerated. However, there are those who still believe, and Pekuleh operates a sort of under-ground magic service, offering us a demonstration for three dollars.

By the scant light of an oil lamp, Pekuleh sat down and pro-duced two dark polished rocks—one with a doughnut hole, the other curved like a small scimitar. He told us that thirty years ago, the first rock was left under his pillow by Anying Ibou, the other in his field house by Lihan Lilling. Both his benefactors were ghosts. And with the rocks he could call the ghosts at will. First he bent his head in prayer and crossed his chest. Then he launched into a crazed chant and seemed to lose himself in a trance. He emptied rice from a tin cup—an offering to the spirits—then showed us that the vessel was empty, using the same melodramatic gestures Las Vegas lounge prestidigitators employ. Then he dropped in the two rocks, rattled them around a bit, and walked outside to the porch. A minute later he returned—with water in the cup!

Pekuleh explained that the water was left by the two ghosts, and that it was magic healing water, sought by the whole community and other villages as well. If a sick person came to him, and he asked the ghost for the water and it didn't appear, the sufferer would die. With its manifestation, all would be hunky-dory, as long as the missionaries weren't told. He sprinkled the water on my head, then blew through his fist that held the rocks, then touched my cheeks. It was over. I was cured. I hadn't felt bad in the first place, I confessed to Taman Kahang, but one never knows.

A powerful rain kept things quiet the next morning, but by noon the sun was shouldering the clouds, and in Long Lebusan warriors were gussying up. The first reenactment was an "open war" on the muddy football field, replete with war masks, argus-pheasant feathers in plaited-fiber, toquelike helmets (worn in the past only by successful headhunters), panther-skinned girdles, flashing *parangs,* and dropping bodies. They refused to say which battle they were reenacting, except that it was intertribal, because it might prove embarrassing. No human blood was spilled, but to give verisimilitude an enormous bleating pig was speared to death, and the field ran red.

At last it was time for the reenactment of the first peace conference, Jalung Apui's seminal council that put the brakes on runaway headhunting. In this conference, Jalung Apui invited the leaders of the four closest Kenyah subtribes to join him. For the reenactment, all of Long Lebusan gathered on a long-house gallery in front of a wall mural depicting two tigers flanking a Chinese vase. Over the vase hovered a hornbill. As in Long Uro, the vase was supposed to hold the souls of all the Kenyah people; the hornbill protected the vase from above, while the two tigers, representing Jalung Apui and his cousin Pingam Sutang, guarded the sides.

An effigy of an enormous hornbill with tinder, a symbol of fire, in his beak, hung from the ceiling joists; it also represented Jalung Apui. The fire would burn to death any chief who didn't stick to the peace pact. Four smaller hornbills ringed the large one, representing the four subtribe chiefs. The reenactment began with Jalung Apui and his fellow chiefs stooping over a trough and slopping up rice, as though they were dogs, to indicate how, as headhunters, they had reduced themselves to animals. An old woman wearing blue then called the chiefs as though they were mongrels, and they turned and rose as humans. Then they cut themselves and dripped their collective blood into a cup, which was passed around for each to take a drink, a blood-brother peace toast. Five tiger's teeth were dipped into the cup, symbolizing that if the chiefs didn't keep the peace pact, a tiger would come and eat their hearts out. This was the beginning of the end. They would return to their respective villages and start the process of winding down the hunting of heads, a conversion that would take more than half a century to realize.

That evening, our last, we were called to the porch for another dance. We expected the graceful Kenyah performances we'd witnessed in Long Uro, and we got them, plus a bit more as well. As the *sambas* were tuned, a man emerged from the shadows down the gallery dragging a big fish trap with a propeller attached. Inside was another man, who spun the propeller as they moved into the light amidst gales of laughter. The man inside the ersatz plane stepped out and stood next to the other. They looked like Taman Kahang and myself—Westerners. They had white chalk covering their faces and hands; they had sharp Western noses, fashioned from cardboard. Their hair was slicked back. They were wearing jeans and backpacks, and one had a fake beard. The other had a tin can on a string slung around his neck, which he pointed toward the audience as though it were a camera.

The burlesque was uncanny, a keen mimicry of their visitors, with mannerisms and tics down to a tee. The man playing me would stop and point his camera at a winsome young girl in an exact impersonation of me. The village was convulsed in laughter, and I was as well, though I also felt I had been dissected and was being held up in a beaker for the class to see. But this was exactly what I had been doing to them for the past two weeks, and what missionaries, colonialists, anthropologists, humanists, and moralists had done for decades before me. I realized I was probably abetting the process Taman Kahang so wanted to arrest—the Westernization and moral deterioration of the Dayaks.

Yes, headhunting was evil. The taking of any human life is evil, the paramount crime against humanity. But, it could be argued, the Dayak Kenyah headhunters had a higher moral philosophy than our own. Our methods of warfare allow us to forget our enemies have names and faces. Although the headhunter on a raid was a treacherous and indiscriminate killer of men, women, and children, there were at least some human as well as technological limits to the brutality of the system. His wars were waged against people who could provide links with the eternal powers of the gods and ancestors. Our wars are fought over an economic system, or oil, or politics, or reasons nobody really understands. And they're fought electronically and with the same strategies used to eliminate vermin.

As the skit was winding down, I looked over to my British host, Taman Kahang, and his Dayak wife, Farida, and noticed something with little significance. After two weeks in the highlands, Taman Kahang was now beginning to look like a Dayak hunter—he was unshaven and unwashed, his face dark with dirt, and he wore the same stained, ripped, and wrinkled clothing he'd started with. Yet Farida, seated next to him, wore a freshly pressed cotton dress, meticulously applied nail polish, a new Seiko watch, and a chic gold necklace. Somehow they'd switched places, and each was striving for what the other had had by birthright.

THE MYTH
OF ADVENTURE

THE MYTH OF ADVENTURE
A Thousand Years of Danger and Derring-do

Whatever you can do, or dream you can, begin it;
Boldness has genius, power and magic in it.

Goethe

If there is a common thread to adventure across the millennium, it is risk. And risk is its greatest asset. At the moment of capsize, the wall clutch, or facing the feral eyes of a forest animal, we are febrile but also unlocked in a way that never happens in the comfort zone, so that the slightest tap makes us shiver to the bottom of our beings. If we survive, it is at this moment that we learn most profoundly, we glug down the lessons of life, and consciousness evolves.

Though risk is woven throughout, the notions of adventure, and the nature of its practitioners, have altered much over the past 1,000 years. Trying to capture an encompassing definition is like trying to catch a lizard by its tail: as soon as you think you've got it, it leaves it in your fingers and grows a new one. Nonetheless, if I were to attempt to corner adventure, I might roughly cast a fence divided into four stages, fashioned by those who personified different ages of adventuring: The Merchant Adventurers; the Passion Adventurers; the Trophy Adventurers; and the Touro-adventurers.

For most of the millennium adventurers were severely financed explorers on expedition, capable souls willing to trade life and limb in the quest of scientific, religious, political, or economic booty for their backers. This was closer to war than romance, in that partici-

212

pants often lived in fear, supped on hard biscuits, sawdust, and rats, and slept lonely on hard surfaces in hopes of returning to a better life a bit richer, perhaps with a promotion and some fame. More often than not, these adventures were distinguished by their accidents, either in geographic discovery or in loss of life; their adventures were, in essence, well-planned trips gone wrong. For the former, there are such well-known misadventureres as Leif Ericsson, who was blown off course during a voyage from Norway to Greenland about A.D. 1000 and instead knocked into North America. Nearly five centuries later, Columbus made history imagining he had arrived in the Indies, when he was in fact half a world away in the Caribbean.

On the fatal front, we remember the adventures of Ferdinand Magellan, who in 1521 was looking for a western trade route to the Spice Islands when he came to a sticky end in a local skirmish in the Philippines; likewise, Ponce de Leon, Brule Etienne, Captain Cook, John Gilbert, and Jedediah Smith were killed by contumacious locals during their explorations. Vitus Bering died of exposure navigating the northern sea that would bear his surname; Henry Hudson disappeared in his namesake bay after he was put adrift in a small boat by a mutinous crew; and Scottish doctor Mungo Park vanished while navigating the Niger River. John Franklin lost his entire expedition, two ships and 129 men, when he became icebound trying to negotiate the Northwest Passage. And while Henry Morton Stanley survived his 999-day journey across the malarial midriff of the Dark Continent, half of his 359 men did not. Robert Falcon Scott may have been a last of breed, sacrificing himself and his party to an Antarctic storm for the sake of science (he dragged rocks and specimens across the continent to within eleven miles of a resupply depot) and of British boasting rights to be the first to the South Pole; in spite of his efforts, Norwegian Roald Amundsen beat him by five weeks.

The point is, these adventures were decidedly dangerous, and, like enlisting to go to battle, those who volunteered had the grim expectation they might not return. The Merchant Adventurers were willing to go where only dragons marked the map, and to tender their lives for queen, country or God, or the trading company. If there was any personal gratification or growth that came from the exercise, it was tangential. The central goal was to survive and come home with bounty, be it new colonies, converted souls, slaves, spices, or knowledge.

The second wave of adventure had its antecedents in Richard Burton, who, though commissioned by the English East India Company, and later, the Royal Geographical Society, really set about exploring to satisfy his own insatiable curiosity about foreign life, languages, and exotic sex. He was a Passion Adventurer, who sought out perfectly unnecessary hazards in the name of inquisitiveness, and pursued exploration not for empire or some larger good, but for his own love of discovery.

Ernest Shackleton was an early executant this century of the Passion Adventurer. For his ill-conceived plan to cross Antarctica he had major sponsors, and promoted his "Imperial" expedition as scientific, though he had no interest in science, even scorned it. The real reasons for the extreme endeavor were personal: He loved a good adventure; loved the romantic notion of searching for treasure; and loved to sing, jig, and joke with his mates in the field. Everything else was an excuse.

Others came to personify this type of adventure in a more direct way, such as New Zealand beekeeper Ed Hillary, who clearly had a vast enthusiasm for climbing and was able to parlay it to membership on a high-profile British Himalayan expedition; and Wilfred Thesiger, who loved the desert, and spent forty years exploring its inner reaches, including a crossing of Arabia's Empty Quarter. When Teddy Roosevelt decided to explore the River of Doubt in Brazil, he said, "I had to go. It was my last chance to be a boy." It was his passion for adventure that took him to the Amazon, where he picked up the malaria that led to his premature death.

The later part of the twentieth century found Arne Rubin, who made the first canoe trip down the Blue Nile; Naomi Uemura, the first to reach the North Pole solo by dogsled; and Robyn Davidson, the first woman to cross the Australian desert by camel. They, too, personified the Passion Adventurers, those who followed some irresistible inner call to find terra incognita and the light that illumes the ground within. Always there was healthy risk involved: The catalogue is thick with those who didn't come back, from George Leigh Mallory to Amelia Earhart and, more recently, Ned Gillette, murdered on a glacier in Pakistan, and Doug Gordon, drowned while attempting a first descent of the Tsangpo Gorge in Tibet.

Like all adventurers, these needed to be financed. Some used the glossy pretexts of flag planting or coloring in the map and found patrons; others paid their way as journalists, photographers, filmmakers, or shills for commercial products or services. And some had the family pocketbook to underwrite their passion for adventure. One of the first of this class most certainly was the pipe-smoking Englishman Samuel Baker, who spent the early 1860s on a stylish, self-financed expedition exploring the watersheds of Abyssinia, camping on Persian rugs beneath double-lined umbrellas as hyenas whooped nearby. A little over a century later, New Jersey native and self-styled adventurer Joel Fogel financed a first raft descent of the crocodiled lower Omo in Ethiopia with family monies. And newspapers in recent years have fawned over the various self-financed balloon adventures of dough-boys Richard Branson and Steve Fossett.

A subgroup of the Passion Adventurers were founders of adventure travel firms a quarter century ago, who discovered they could fund their global rummagings in the name of seeking out new adventures for an emerging clientele who would follow in the footsteps of a packaging explorer. I confess, I was one such entrepreneurial explorer.

In the late 1960s, after scraping together enough change to make some first rafting descents along rivers of the eastern seaboard, I knew that running new rivers would be my life-long compulsion. I rolled out a map of the world and drooled at all the fresh, turning water that had yet to be navigated. So, with some like-minded friends, I started a trifling company we named Sobek Expeditions, with ambitions to carom down all the wild rivers of the planet, using other people's money. The formula was simple: Use the company coffers to fund an exploratory rafting expedition; assuming the expedition was replicable (and more than a few times it was not), write up an itinerary, print a brochure, and offer the retracing as a commercial trip, hiring Colorado River guides to run the excursion; use the profits from the commercial tour to fund another exploratory endeavor, in an Endless Summer cycle. My narcotic was the adventure of rafting where none had gone before, and I rarely returned for a second descent. But a certain sort of client did: the Trophy Adventurer.

The Trophy Adventurers were early adopters, alpha-seekers, calculated risk takers, dilettantes who collected experiences, but didn't want to be involved in the fuss of planning and organization, or the extreme danger of being first; they wanted to be professionally guided. This type of adventure was invented in the Romantic era with the first guided trips to Mont Blanc, and perhaps the first adventure travel company, the Chamonix-based Compagnie des Guides, was formed to accommodate these new holiday doings.

Ernest Hemingway was certainly of this ilk, with his guided safaris and fishing expeditions; Dick Bass and Sandy Hill Pittman are more modern examples, having paid dearly to have guides get them up the Seven Summits. And there were hundreds others who would pay to follow Lars-Eric Lindblad to Easter Island, or Leo LeBon to Nepal, or John Yost and myself down the Bio-Bio or the Zambezi. These adventurers, who expected discomfort, challenge, and risk to earn their prizes, fueled the beginnings of American-based adventure travel companies, including Mountain Travel, Abercrombie & Kent, and Sobek Expeditions. As outfitters pioneering a new type of travel, we practically guaranteed that something would go wrong: Our place of business was the wilderness, which is always in flux and ever dangerous; routes were untested, infrastructures didn't exist, GPSs weren't around for geodetic bearings, and cell phones and the Internet weren't available for instant information. But that was okay; our clients, the Trophy Adventurers, didn't care. When there was a screw-up, when we got lost, more often than not there was exhilaration, not damnation.

I remember a watershed moment when things began to change. Up into the early 1980s, the adventure travel business was a niche enterprise, a gimmicky subset of the vacation industry catering to the Trophy Adventurers and not much more. My partners and I pretty much lived hand to mouth, but that didn't matter, as we were traveling the globe and digging up the doubloons of personal adventures. I lived in a bunkhouse near the office, took no salary, and had a passport with so many accordion pages it was fat as a paperback. And the relationship I had with our clients was wonderfully symbiotic and respectful. Though the Trophy Adventurers were often motivated by the chance to go one better, or at least one showier, than their neighbors, I realized they had a keen conviction that in that last decade of the millennium we had become too remote from our beginnings, too remote from Nature, too remote from the innocent landscapes that lie within ourselves. These adventures we offered were a chance to pluck at the strings of simplicity again, to strip the veneer of the worldliness that made these people successful and return them to some more primitive, if more demanding, state of grace.

But one day in the early 1980s, a twist of fate with broad downstream effects happened in the road. Curt Smith, a young man with a business background, was driving down California Highway 49 when he made a bad turn in front of the Sobek offices, got into an accident, and had to stick around while his car got fixed. While waiting, he became a guide. A few months later, in the fall of 1983, Curt suggested we have an "offsite" to discuss the future of the company. So, the weekend following, Curt, my partners, some top guides, and I retreated to the cramped Sonora living room of Paul Henry, our accountant, and rolled out our sleeping bags on the floor for two days of planning. Mostly we talked about new places to go, and new activities to try. But at one pivotal moment, Curt challenged us and said, "Don't you want to make money?" John Yost was quick to reply: "No! We're in this for the adventure, not for money."

But Curt kept pushing, and by the end of the weekend, we had agreed to a new concept—something we would call "soft adventure." The idea was to produce an adventure tour for the masses, and that meant an itinerary that was comfortable, easy, inexpensive, reliable, and accessible. Three months later we began mailing a new brochure entitled "Andean Odyssey: 9 days from just $999—Airfare included!" There were thirteen departures, all identical, all featuring easy walks, a bouncy raft ride through the Sacred Valley of the Incas, and a scenic train ride to Machu Picchu. But unlike adventures past wherein participants camped, ate freeze-dried food or what could be caught or picked, and pushed themselves physically and emotionally, in this iteration the participants stayed in inns each night, with hot showers, cold drinks, clean sheets, and insect- and moonlight-free. The offering was wildly successful, and adventure was forever changed: It was commoditized! Born was the Touro-adventurer, boldly going where hundreds, perhaps thousands, had gone before.

Well, comfort in the wilds had been around for some time, but it had mostly been for the moneyed class. This offering was among the first that addressed a mainstream audience, and relied upon low margins and high numbers to become a business. It worked, and the Sobek catalogue was suddenly chock-full of soft adventures, and our intrepid guides were escorting knots of blue rinses, charm bracelets, and natty safari jackets among the glaciers and rain forests. A hundred adventure companies sprung to life with the concept of taking Touro-adventurers into the back of beyond with the same consistency and creature comforts as a Caribbean cruise or a European bus tour. Now, if there were an unexpected change in itinerary, or rain when the brochure suggested sunshine, or if the orangutans didn't show their faces on schedule, or the eco-lodge had ants, the Touro-adventurer asked for a refund. When something went wrong, there was little serendipity; there were lawsuits. Chance, like a bone in the desert, was bleached from the landscape.

Letting the Touro-adventurer out of the box was a mixed blessing, though. For me, it meant a compromise, watering a pure product down for the hoi polloi, rejiggering my company for a lower common denominator, concentrating more on streamlining current offerings rather than cobbling together exploratories. But it also meant better wages for the guides and staff, health insurance, 401K plans, and tents with working zippers, and it meant sharing the obeahism of adventure with more people, and that was a good thing.

When Ed Hillary spoke out against commercial climbs up Everest, his words rang with remorse for a season lost to time: "How thankful I was that I was active in a pioneering era when we established the route, carried the loads, all worked together for the ultimate objective. The way things are now, I don't think I would have bothered." Today, with Passion Adventurers looking backwards, we hear the same cry: that those who climbed a mountain or ran an unrun river before the advent of adventure shepherds, GPSs, and connections to the Web were the real pioneers, with a much more authentic experience. Many have complained that Yosemite, the Grand Canyon, Kilimanjaro, and Victoria Falls have lost some transcendence because of their manufactured and commercial accessibility, and that the backcountry is no longer so if one can call for help on a cell phone. Some, though, say it is elitist to deny others what a Passion Adventurer may have experienced, to preserve in private sanctuary the epiphany that came with a special effort, time, and place. In my years as a river guide I escorted blind children, senior citizens, and paraplegics down the Colorado River, and I can testify that the transformational aspects of the experience were as vital for them as for the young, hearty, do-it-yourself expeditioneers. It may be less of a feat now to climb Everest than in 1953, what with better gear, communications technology, and routes well described, but adventure is a relative experience, one that has morphed through the ages, and is interpreted on an individual basis. The sense of exhilaration and achievement is really no less for the guided Trophy Adventurer today who stretches her ice ax above the summit of

Everest as it was for Ed Hillary. And those same exalted feelings are just as powerful and genuine for the Touro-adventurer who pitches his first tent or lights his first campfire, looks his first leopard in the eye, or takes his first canyoning jaunt in Switzerland. All have taken risks, and if they survived, they reaped rewards.

Besides, it is the Touro-adventurer who may save the wilderness world for the rest of us, and it is in the theater of wilderness where the risk of adventure is played. The ledger is long of wilderness areas gone down because there wasn't a constituency to do the battle. Glen Canyon of the Colorado River is the poster child. A basic problem has been that wilderness areas are traditionally hard to get to, and the numbers who saw them, experienced them, and fell in love with them were too often too small to make a difference. That's where the companies that cater to the Touro-adventurers come in, as instruments of awareness, appreciation, and activism— a result of green-bonding, as some now call it—that no feature in the pages of *National Geographic* magazine ever could. When time comes for a call to action to stop the drowning of a wild river, the patronage for preservation is that much greater for the Touro-adventurers who have been escorted to the magic places and been touched by what they saw and felt, even if they did expect a flush toilet at the campsite. A couple years ago we lost a fight to save Chile's crown jewel of a wild river, the Bio-Bio, from the concrete slug of a private big dam; but then only a few thousand had ever seen the river. Now more people in the United States raft on a hot weekend than visit the Smithsonian, and that means there will be that many more who fall in love with a wild river, who understand its issues, and will lend a hand when needed. But that doesn't mean I am optimistic about where adventure seems to be headed.

Now, according to a U.S. Data Center study, more than half of all U.S. traveling adults (about 73 million folks) have taken an adventure trip in their lifetime. There is now something called the Adventure Travel Business Trade Association, and it claims there are around eight thousand American companies packaging tours for adventure, earning some $7 billion annually. One can become an ersatz Indiana Jones, complete with khakis and fedora, with a click-through to any of a thousand outfitters on the Web. The definition of adventure keeps widening and stretching. Indoor climbing walls, often not far from a real rock face, are a rage. Universal Studios' new $2.7 billion theme park, *Islands of Adventure*, is a huge hit, with such offerings as white-water raft trips down Dudley Do-Right's Ripsaw Falls. The tyranny of geography can be cut away with interactive virtual adventures, transmitted in real time from the field via the Web, yet experienced in a climate-controlled cube through the portal of a computer screen, or in the living room through interactive TV.

How will people take their adventures in the next millennium? I would bet that Philip K. Dick's vision of buying memories, as portrayed by Arnold Schwarzenegger in the movie *Total Recall*, will apply to adventure as well: You visit your local travel agency, buy the "Climb Everest" implant, and emerge minutes later with a complete memory of the grand adventure—all without a Khumbu cough, pulmonary edema, toes lost to frostbite, snoring tent mates, or any element of peril or fear. Adventure will become the logical conclusion of where it is headed. . . . Wrinkle-free, washed clean of any speck of risk, nothing more than an inconvenience wrongly considered, nothing more than a myth.

But, if you will believe in the paradigm of High-Tech, High-Touch . . . meaning that the more technology takes over the tasks of life, the more we will covet the touch of a real experience, then there is hope, there is hope. The outfitters, the operators, the guides; those who can offer the sweat, the sunburn, the aches, the insect bites, and the risk of things going wrong alongside the cool caress of a wave, the warm sun on the back, the view that drops the jaw, all without a link to civilization—these are the saviors of adventure, the souls and spirits who will usher in the next phase of adventure, and with it, the evolution of consciousness, and perhaps the preservation of the real world.

ABOUT THE AUTHOR

An international explorer, entrepreneur, internet pioneer, and award-winning author, Richard Bangs has dedicated much of his career to adventure and wilderness travel. He led first descents of thirty-five rivers, including the Yangtze in China and Zambezi in Africa. Bangs is a founding partner of Mountain Travel-Sobek, American's oldest and largest adventure travel firm.

In 1996, he served as Editor-in-Chief of *Mungo Park,* Expedia.com's online adventure travel magazine. From 1999 to 2001, Bangs was also Editor-at-Large for Expedia, Inc. He has been a contributing editor to MSNBC, a guest lecturer at the Smithsonian Institute, the National Geographic Society, the Explorer's Club, the Denver Museum of Natural History, and many other notable venues.

Bangs is currently the president of Outward Bound USA, the nation's leading force in experiential education.

Bangs' publishing credits include more than 500 magazine articles, 13 books. His book *The Lost River: A Memoir of Life, Death, and Transformation of Wild Water* (Sierra Club/Random House) won the 1999 National Book Award for Outdoor Literature and the Lowell Thomas Award for Best Travel Book of 1999.

THE MOUNTAINEERS, founded in 1906, is a nonprofit outdoor activity and conservation club, whose mission is "to explore, study, preserve, and enjoy the natural beauty of the outdoors. . . . " Based in Seattle, Washington, the club is now the third-largest such organization in the United States, with 15,000 members and five branches throughout Washington State.

The Mountaineers sponsors both classes and year-round outdoor activities in the Pacific Northwest, which include hiking, mountain climbing, ski-touring, snowshoeing, bicycling, camping, kayaking and canoeing, nature study, sailing, and adventure travel. The club's conservation division supports environmental causes through educational activities, sponsoring legislation, and presenting informational programs. All club activities are led by skilled, experienced volunteers, who are dedicated to promoting safe and responsible enjoyment and preservation of the outdoors.

If you would like to participate in these organized outdoor activities or the club's programs, consider a membership in The Mountaineers. For information and an application, write or call The Mountaineers, Club Headquarters, 300 Third Avenue West, Seattle, WA 98119; 206-284-6310.

The Mountaineers Books, an active, nonprofit publishing program of the club, produces guidebooks, instructional texts, historical works, natural history guides, and works on environmental conservation. All books produced by The Mountaineers Books fulfill the club's mission.

Send or call for our catalog of more than 500 outdoor titles:

The Mountaineers Books
1001 SW Klickitat Way, Suite 201
Seattle, WA 98134
800-553-4453
mbooks@mountaineersbooks.org
www.mountaineersbooks.org

Other titles you might enjoy from The Mountaineers Books

Available at fine bookstores and outdoor stores, by phone at 800-553-4453, or on the World Wide Web at www.mountaineersbooks.org.

Chomolungma Sings the Blues by Ed Douglas. $14.95 paperback. 0-89886-843-2.

Escape Routes: Further Adventure Writings of David Roberts by David Roberts. $16.95 paperback. 0-89886-601-4.

Where the Pavement Ends: One Woman's Bicycle Trip Through Mongolia, China & Vietnam by Erika Warmbrunn. $24.95 hardcover. 0-89886-684-7.

Spirited Waters: Soloing South Through the Inside Passage by Jennifer Hahn. $24.95 hardcover. 0-89886-744-4.

Miles From Nowhere: A Round-the-World Bicycle Adventure by Barbara Savage. $14.95 paperback. 0-89886-109-8.

On Top of the World: Five Women Explorers in Tibet by Luree Miller. $12.95 paperback. 0-89886-097-0.

Ghosts of Everest: The Search for Mallory & Irvine by Jochen Hemmleb, Larry A. Johnson, and Eric R. Simonson. $24.95 paperback. 0-89886-850-5.

In the Zone: Epic Survival Stories From the Mountaineering World by Peter Potterfield. $16.95 paperback. 0-89886-568-9.

The Mountaineers Anthology Series: Glorious Failures, Volume I edited by The Mountaineers Books Staff. $16.95 paperback. 0-89886-825-4.

The Falling Season: Inside the Life and Death Drama of Aspen's Mountain Rescue Team by Hal Clifford. $16.95 paperback. 0-89886-633-2.

The Burgess Book of Lies by Adrian and Alan Burgess. $24.95 paperback. 0-89886-641-3.

Stone Palaces by Geof Childs. $16.95 paperback. 0-89886-851-3.

Postcards From the Ledge: Collected Mountaineering Writings of Greg Child by Greg Child. $16.95 paperback. 0-89886-753-3.